NINE LIVES

Published by MomentBooks
Copyright © 2011 by Center for Creative Change
All Rights Reserved

MomentBooks is an imprint of Moment Magazine, a division of
Center for Creative Change, Washington, DC

For information about permission to reproduce selections from this book,
write to MomentBooks c/o Center for Creative Change,
4115 Wisconsin Avenue, NW,
Suite LL10, Washington, DC 20016, momentmag.com.

For information about special discounts for bulk purchases or author
events, please contact MomentBooks at marketing@momentmag.com or
(202)363-6425.

Library of Congress Cataloguing-in-Publication Data
*Nine Lives: Favorite Profiles of Famous People from the Annals of Moment
Magazine* edited by Marcy Epstein and Nadine Epstein
p. cm.

ISBN 978-0-9839951-0-4 (soft cover)

1. Jews—Biography 2. Biography 3. Jews—United States—Identity 4.

Judaism—General
2011   BM750-755   AC1-999   AC200   BM1-449

Some material originally appeared in *Moment Magazine*, 2007-2011.

This book is produced on paper recycled from post-consumer materials,

10 9 8 7 6 5 4 3 2 1

Manufactured in the United States of America

Cover design by: Navid Marvi

Cover Photos: Jon Stewart: AP Images; Albert Einstein: Getty Images; Bob Dylan: Creative Commons; Walter Mosley: David Burnett/courtesy of Penguin Group; Ruth Bader Ginsburg: AP Images; Sergey Brin: Courtesy of Google; Brian Epstein: Newscom; Tony Kushner: AP Images; Oliver Sacks: Adam Scourfield/courtesy of Oliver Sacks.

Profile Photos: Albert Einstein, pg. 12: Creative Commons; Ruth Bader Ginsburg, pg.34: Creative Commons; Sergey Brin, pg.42: Courtesy of Google; Tony Kushner, pg. 60: Gloria Wegener/courtesy of Tony Kushner; Jon Stewart, pg. 70: Adam M. Stump/Creative Commons; Walter Mosley, pg. 86: David Burnett/courtesy of Penguin Group; Bob Dylan, pg. 96: Creative Commons; Brian Epstein, pg. 110: Newscom; Oliver Sacks, pg. 130: Adam Scourfield/courtesy of Oliver Sacks

To Steven
Enjoy!
Nadine Epstein

NINE LIVES

FAVORITE PROFILES OF FAMOUS PEOPLE
FROM THE ANNALS OF MOMENT MAGAZINE

EDITORS

Marcy Epstein and Nadine Epstein

FOREWORD   **AFTERWORD**

Sidney Offit   *Gloria Steinem*

m

MomentBooks
Washington, DC

In Memory of Warren Dennis

TABLE OF CONTENTS

FOREWORD

In the Talmud, rabbis intensely scrutinized Jewish life and ritual while discussing everything from anatomy, biology, botany, zoology and medicine to astrology. They spun creative legal fictions to explain their positions and told extravagant stories to prove their points. They applied cold logic to determine who could or could not be a Jew, and evolved complex theorems to calculate what a person could or could not do on Shabbat.

No wonder that for millennia, the rabbinate attracted the brightest minds. But over the last several centuries, the Talmud has become one of many compelling intellectual paths as Jews have poured their energy into the arts, the law, science and a wide range of academic scholarship and commercial disciplines. I call this phenomenon "displaced Talmudic energy."

What is this energy? Certainly it must fuel what we call intellect. Karl Marx, for example, funneled his intellectual energy into creating an entire political-economic structure. Sigmund Freud, the father of psychoanalysis, thought vigorously about the architecture of the mind. For these creative giants and many others, intellect was a consuming fire.

That same fire consumes the extraordinary Jewish scientists, entrepreneurs, champions of law, theater, literature and the performing arts profiled in this collection. And it remains a Jewish fire in that each sketch focuses on the private relationship of the subject to his or her identity as a Jew. The ever-present question is: How has he or she taken Judaism and reshaped it to a new discipline?

The volume kicks off with Albert Einstein, a man clearly indebted to Talmudic questioning. Approaching science, he asks, "Why?" and comes up with a way of envisioning and ordering the universe while considering that he could well be missing something or be wrong. And no bolder definition of the simplicity of Jewish identity exists than that expressed by this great mind. At a Purim dinner before an American audience in 1935, when reports of Nazi brutalities to German Jews were filtering through the international news web, the Nobel Laureate declared: "There are no German Jews; there are no Russian Jews; there are no American Jews. Their only difference is their daily language. There are in fact only Jews."

Of course, there is no clearer legacy of Talmudic law than the modern legal system as mastered by Ruth Bader Ginsburg. The illuminating portrait of this Supreme Court Justice affirms that she continues to identify as a Jew and feels pleased that her grandchildren do, too. "This is a heritage that you can be proud of," she says. She tells, however, how as a teenager, she was offended by the exclusion of women from so much of Jewish ritual. "When my mother died," she remembers, "the house was filled with women; but only men could participate in the minyan [the quorum required for public prayer]." I suspect Justice Ginsburg's feelings are epidemic among many intelligent Jewish women. She follows the tradition of many who question the rituals, yet feel proud of the religion and its intellectual legacy.

The Talmud's attention to detail can also be found in vast reordering of information made possible by the algorithms that Sergey Brin and fellow Jewish computer geek and entrepreneur, Larry Page, created as the basis of their civilization-changing company, Google. Brin emigrated from Russia to the United States with his father and mother when he was a child. Among Brin's enthusiasms for life in America was "…the discovery that they were free to be Jews." By the age of 33, the co-founder of Google was estimated to be a multi-billionaire.

Playwright Tony Kushner is unafraid to be an outspoken public intellectual at a time when few are willing to risk the consequences. Through his plays, he attempts to reshape Judaism for a new era by challenging accepted thinking, a signature of rabbinic tradition. A Pulitzer Prize winner, Kushner grew up in Lake Charles, Louisiana, where his family belonged to a Reform temple. "So Reform," Kushner quips, "that it was virtually reformed out of existence." Kushner's religious practice is defined by his assertion that he rejects the parts of Judaism that seem like "repression cloaked in a religious disguise" and embraces those that appeal to him. When he married editor Mark Harris, he insisted a rabbi preside. "I wanted to be married under a chuppa. I wanted to say the blessings. I wanted there to be Hebrew."

Along the lines of a modern day Talmudist, Jon Stewart parses not text but the spoken words and actions of powerful media personalities, politicians, pundits and other public figures in contemporary society. Born Jonathan Stuart Leibowitz, the host of *The Daily Show* on cable TV's Comedy Central is frequently cited as a master of Jewish humor and routinely reminds his audience that he is Jewish. While "he rarely speaks earnestly about his Jewish upbringing or what being Jewish means to him," being Jewish is a part of who is he is and is something with which he is at ease. With his unspoken mission of making the world a better place, he has more than once been called America's most beloved "rabbi."

Walter Mosley, an intellectual dynamo, takes on a question that has fascinated Jewish scholars for centuries and still remains relevant today: Who is a Jew? High priest of letters—novels, essays, political "manifestos"—Mosley is the son of an intellectual Jewish mother and a father whom he defines as "a black Socrates." His reflection on ethnic and religious identity is authentic and unusual. Declaring Jews to be a race, he says: "Every kind of ethnicity is great with me. If it's soul food or kreplach, I'm going to eat it."

Bob Dylan is not normally thought of as an intellectual but as an intuitively talented artist, yet as his profile tracks in detail, a vast amount of energy permeates his relationship with religion and his lifelong determination to come to some kind of truth with which he can live. The Minnesota-born folk singer who was acclaimed the "poet of a generation" has spent his life on a perpetual spiritual quest, one which led him away from Judaism and then back. Born Robert Zimmerman, he was the son of a local B'nai Brith leader and a Hadassah president: His fascinating journey took him from Wisconsin's Herzl Camp to a mystical communion with Jesus, then to Israel for his son's bar mitzvah at the Western Wall and a deepening relationship with Judaism.

The Talmud is known for judging sages by their students, and by this standard, Brian Epstein, a Liverpool Jew who was the manager of *The Beatles*, is unparalleled. We read with wonder about this ultimate outsider—due to his Orthodox Jewish upbringing and homosexuality—who became mentor to the most iconic band of the last century. He was the group's friend and "enabler" who with fierce integrity and gracious style guided them to world fame and great fortune. When Epstein died of a drug overdose at an early age, *The Beatles* attended the memorial service at the New London Synagogue. "All four wore black paper yarmulkes."

Appropriately enough, this galactic academy of 20th century Jewish heroes launches with a profile of Albert Einstein and concludes with an interview of Oliver Sacks, a physician, scientist and master of the narrative text. The book returns full circle to the core of Talmudic Judaism, questioning, the inspiration for Sacks' scientific inquiries. We are introduced to Sacks with the words, "according to family lore, Sacks' grandfathers were so Orthodox that one would wake up at night if his yarmulka slipped off his head while the other would not swim without his." Sacks, although willing to confess to a love of pumpernickel bagels "topped with herring," is reluctant to talk to people about religion, anymore than he would talk about sex. Yet he finds Hebrew, which he knows intimately, to be a sacred language.

What is one to conclude from this montage, this scintillating mosaic of contemporary and historical Jewish achievers that fuses scholarship and one-on-one interviews? Certainly these sketches are testimony to diverse interpretations of Jewish belief. I suggest that as you read, you are likely to experience an epiphany of "reader identity." Perhaps you'll be moved by Ruth Bader Ginsburg's discomfort with the secondary role of women in prayer services, or Tony Kushner's demand for same-sex inclusion in the Jewish ritual of marriage, or Jon Stewart's high standards of human behavior, or Bob Dylan's embrace of Orthodox Judaism, or Sergey Brin's pride in the Jewish intellectual tradition. Or it may be that, like me, you are most moved by the bonds forged by millennia of persecution: Einstein's "Born a Jew, always a Jew" belief. Regardless, all should delight in these brilliant portraits of the doubts, challenges and fiercely artful "displacements of Talmudic energy."

Sidney Offit
New York, New York, 2011

1

WAS EINSTEIN A JEWISH SAINT?

Mandy Katz • *April/May 2007*

As usual, Albert Einstein hadn't dressed for the occasion. Most of the forty or so young men waiting for him that Friday night in January at Princeton's Murray-Dodge Hall sported the "college man's" uniform of 1947—their best tweed sport coats and shined loafers. But their guest of honor, when he finally showed up, was wearing a baggy sweatshirt, soft-soled slippers and no socks.

Einstein padded to the front of the room to give a short talk—not about the theory of relativity, special or general, or even the unified field theory he was currently working on at the nearby Institute for Advanced Study. Rather, Einstein had a few words to share about the importance of identifying as a Jew. He "stressed that it was important for Jews to be part of a Jewish community," a student would later recall in his notes on the event. "He believed that it was important for all Jews to have Jewish friends."

This was a radical idea at a school that, under its officially non-existent quota system in the 1940s, admitted only 25 Jews into each 750-person class. Less than a decade earlier, in 1938 and 1939, incoming Princeton freshmen asked in a survey to name the "greatest living person" had ranked Einstein second to Adolf Hitler both years.

"There was a certain number of Jewish students who, when asked, 'What is your religion?' wrote 'no religion,'" says 83-year-old Ernest Stock, who organized the student meeting. "Whether for good reasons or bad," another student recalls, "we were very reticent about advertising our identities." Stock, a sophomore at the time, had asked Einstein to help inaugurate this gathering of Princeton's Student Hebrew Association. The world's most famous Jew, he knew, could lure his fellow Jews out from behind their tweedy camouflage.

The evening's gathering was an intimate one that began with a Shabbat service led by a guest rabbi before a makeshift ark. The guest of honor stayed afterwards to drink tea and chat with the students, even posing for pictures and signing autographs. It was a cozy affair with nonetheless heady significance. For the first time, Princeton's Jewish undergraduates would no longer have to attend Christian services to fulfill their compulsory chapel requirement. For the first time, Jews would be graced with a room of their own in Murray-Dodge, the university's religious affairs building.

With Einstein's help, Stock and his friends had launched a quiet revolution on the pastoral campus of flagstone footpaths and stately stone buildings. "He was a revered figure and all the Jewish students, particularly, viewed him as a semi-God," says Robert Bloom, 77, who would assume the presidency of the Jewish group in 1950. Einstein's participation had inflated more than attendance, Bloom notes. "For students with doubts about their identity, he just added his great moral prestige."

As he did all over the world throughout his later years, Einstein raised his torch of fame that night to light his listeners' way through a thicket of assimilationist culture. He shared with them a Jewish affinity that sprang not from racial or tribal consciousness—he abhorred parochial allegiances based on blood ties or nationhood—nor from a common faith or set of practices. He perceived, rather, independence of thought and an ethical imperative as the distinct blessings of Jewish heritage, says physics professor Hanoch Gutfreund, former president of Hebrew University in Jerusalem.

The great physicist was a model for Jews of his time. "Not only did he not make it a secret," Gutfreund explains, "but Einstein was proud of his ethnic origin, of belonging, which he perceived as a cultural tradition based on moral values, a long tradition of learning and the pursuit of truth."

For Melvin Antell, 81, a student in Murray-Dodge that night, the message was simpler: "We thought of him as being the outstanding American-Jew. That's what we were: We were Americans. We were Jewish. And with him it all came together."

. . .

EINSTEIN HADN'T BEEN all that different from the Princeton students with whom he sipped tea. He was born in 1879 into an assimilated upper-middle-class family in Ulm in southern Germany. As a young man, when asked his religion on official documents, Einstein would fill in "none," though race-conscious bureaucrats in turn-of-the-century Europe repeatedly required him to change "none" to "Mosaic," a term for Jews.

"Albert's father was proud of the fact that Jewish rites were not practiced in his home," wrote Abraham Pais, an Einstein colleague who authored the Einstein biography *Subtle is the Lord*. Hermann and Pauline Einstein even sent their son to the Catholic school within walking distance of their home, where he was his class's only Jewish student. His teacher once illuminated a lesson on the crucifixion by displaying a huge iron nail, but Einstein never recalled suffering the barbs of anti-Semitism as a child. His sister Maja, however, blessed perhaps with a sharper memory (or thinner skin), described her big brother not only as awkward but also as a playground outcast.

Under a Bavarian law calling for every child to be schooled in his family's religious tradition, Einstein took up home studies in Judaism. Punctilious in their observance of the law, if not religion, Pauline and Hermann retained a distant cousin to tutor 10-year-old Albert in Hebrew, Torah and the teachings of the prophets. To their chagrin, the boy fell in love with God.

Delighted by the idea that human actions could please God, Einstein offered up devotionals in the form of ecstatic paeans that he sang on his way to school. He also gave up eating pork. His parents must have been relieved when geometry began to absorb Albert's attention at age 12. Riveted by Euclid's perfect proofs and order, he soon forsook Jewish ritual and shifted his devotion to science.

As Walter Isaacson, author of *Einstein: His Life and Universe*, observes, Einstein would never return to conventional Jewish practice or belief. "Einstein rebels against religious dogma and becomes a free thinker, but he's still awed by nature and has a religious feeling of awe about the creation of the cosmos," Isaacson says. Rather than become a bar mitzvah, Einstein transferred his religious fervor to the workings of the physical world.

Several years later when, as a brooding teenager, he was thrust out of the family home in Munich, Einstein lost a different sort of paradise, with its tree-filled courtyard where he had tumbled with cousins and observed nature at work. Business reversals had forced the property's sale; Einstein was sent to live in a boarding house to finish his all-important gymnasium education, while his parents and Maja made a fresh start in Italy.

It was more than he could take. Lonely and repelled by what he considered his school's brute, repressive atmosphere and Germany's martial fervor, he was appalled at the prospect of having to enlist in the German army on his impending 16th birthday. To spare himself, in 1894 he abandoned Germany to join his family. By surrendering his passport, he dodged classification as a deserter, opting for statelessness over military service. "That a man can take pleasure in marching in formation to the strains of a band is enough to make me despise him," he would later say.

This raucous, moustached bon vivant appeared to his contemporaries to be both darkly romantic and dangerously disheveled. That, at least, was the opinion of two young Serbian women at the Polytech who began to resent the boisterous German after he captured the heart of their friend and compatriot, Mileva Maric. Maric, two years older than Einstein, was the only woman in his five-member class of physics majors.

The two lovers shared coffee, sausages and pillow talk that meandered from the molecular properties of gases to how to deal with Mother Einstein, who deplored their affair. Pauline objected not because Maric wasn't Jewish; indeed, she had encouraged his previous sweetheart, who was also a Gentile. "It was just marrying an older, brooding, depressive, limping Serbian woman physicist that she wasn't thrilled about," Isaacson explains. Einstein, however, stayed loyal to his dark-haired "dollie," as he called her. Their tumultuous affair led, in 1902, to the birth of an illegitimate daughter, Lieserl, whom Einstein never met. (The scant paper trail indicates she either died as a toddler or was given up for adoption.)

Though the relationship consumed them both, only Maric's professional aspirations would be sacrificed to the conflagration. Einstein's own career, however, almost failed to take off after his graduation in 1900. During two years of miserable joblessness, he at first suspected an unsympathetic professor from the Polytechnic was sabotaging his quest for an academic post in Switzerland. But, when applications also failed farther afield, he began to surmise his "Mosaic" background was holding him back.

One bright spot in these tumultuous years was Switzerland's bestowal of citizenship on Einstein in 1901, once he had satisfactorily demonstrated a sound mind and solid economic prospects. Enamored of the country's tolerant culture and its geopolitical neutrality, he would remain a Swiss citizen throughout his life, even as he changed continents and swore additional allegiances. In 1902, through the intervention of friends, Einstein at last found a job—not the teaching post he had trained for, but a nevertheless satisfactory position in the Swiss patent office, enabling his long-awaited marriage to Maric.

The new Swiss citizen seemed to enjoy patent-examination work. Embarking on a period of astonishingly fertile intellectual activity, he used idle time at his stool and at home to pursue calculations leading to his major scientific breakthroughs of 1905: five stunning articles that included introductions of the photoelectric effect (for which he would win a Nobel Prize in 1921) and the special theory of relativity. That space and time could bend, that acceleration is equivalent to gravity and that $e=mc^2$ were ideas that would change the world, leading to everything from global positioning systems to supermarket laser-scanners to the atom bomb. Einstein was discovering not only new scientific concepts, but a fresh way of conceptualizing the universe and its forces, and beginning to perceive a natural order that had eluded his predecessors.

In his family, however, order was breaking down. As Einstein's star rose among colleagues and academicians, Maric, by 1910 the mother of two sons, saw the light dimming in her own, now entirely domestic world. Closed off from his work, she grew jealous, angering her husband when she intercepted letters between him and a previous girlfriend. The exchange had been innocent, as Einstein insisted, but Maric's suspicions weren't unfounded. She knew from experience how promiscuous her husband could be. Their own romance was long over, and Einstein increasingly treated Maric like a housekeeper and scold rather than the scientific playmate of earlier days.

By 1908, Einstein's continuing discoveries had launched him into the ranks of academia. If it can be said that the stereotype of the "absent-minded professor" didn't actually originate with Einstein, he already looked the part, dashing from lecture to café to apartment with his shirts misbuttoned and collars missing, and having apparently given up on taming or trimming his dark, flyaway mane. His long-dreamed-of professorship at the

University of Zurich was secured in 1909, only after Einstein's faculty sponsor assured the hiring committee that the candidate lacked such known "Israelite" traits as "intrusiveness, impudence, and a shopkeeper's mentality."

Einstein moved to the German University of Prague for a teaching stint that lasted only a year in 1911 but, quite unexpectedly, opened new vistas onto his Jewishness. Taken aback by the snobbery of the Czech-German bourgeoisie and their deliberate segregation from countrymen of Czech and Jewish descent, Einstein sought more amiable society in the city's urbane salon culture, largely driven by highly cultured Jews he called "philosophical and Zionist enthusiasts." He wandered the streets of the city's once-crowded Jewish ghetto, which had been almost entirely razed ten years earlier in an urban renewal initiative. In the historic walled cemetery—centuries of graves beneath hundreds of tombstones arrayed chock-a-block, like crooked teeth—and within the few synagogues that remained, he came across the original bearded inhabitants, clothed in the black garb of their ancient patrimony. When they were to appear on his metaphorical doorstep in Berlin a few years later, Einstein would recognize them as his brothers.

· · ·

IN 1913, A DELEGATION FROM BERLIN, the red-hot center of the physics world, lured Einstein back to Germany. Their inducements to forsake Zurich included a post without teaching duties at the University of Berlin, directorship of his own physics institute at the burgeoning Kaiser Wilhelm Institute and induction as the youngest member of the Prussian Academy of Sciences. Einstein would also be joining, as colleague and collaborator, the world's scientific elite—a high-minded cohort, he imagined, so different from the narrow-minded, spit-and-polish Prussians he had forsaken in his teens.

He and his family followed these sirens to Germany in the summer of 1914. For Maric, however, the music fell flat. She and the boys returned to Zurich within weeks; the four would never again live together as a family. Einstein wept at parting from his sons but could no longer abide their mother. In one of his less vitriolic letters, he described her as "an employee I cannot fire." That the letter was to his mistress didn't help matters. Einstein and Elsa Löwenthal, a divorcée five years older and his second cousin, had been corresponding and meeting illicitly since 1912. Löwenthal's presence in Berlin had added a descant to the Kaiser Institutes' siren song.

Einstein strung Löwenthal along for years while he wrangled with Maric over divorce terms and clung to the pleasures of bachelor life—with Löwenthal now in Maric's place as cook and caretaker. Einstein finally did succeed in "firing" her in 1918. Before succumbing to a second marriage the following year, though, he inflicted on his future wife the ultimate insult of suggesting, quite seriously, that perhaps he should marry her 20-year-old daughter instead. With the callousness of the utterly self-absorbed, he left it to them to decide. "Fortunately" for Löwenthal, the girl opposed the match, so her mother and Einstein tied the knot.

Plump and graying at 45, Löwenthal clucked and fussed over her husband but no longer excited him. Yet, he needed her. Einstein would come to regard his second wife like a favorite pair of slippers—comfortable and even indispensable around the house, but he still wore other shoes. Toward Maric, he gradually mellowed. And with their sons, he managed a loving, albeit complicated, relationship.

As ever, Einstein's personal sturm und drang only enhanced his concentration on work. In the early teens, while Germany "marched in formation" toward the Great War's bloody trenches, he entered possibly the most productive period of his life, writing, lecturing, theorizing and, most notably, making the leap from his 1905 insights into special relativity to the release, in 1916, of his theory of general relativity. Accounting for the effects of gravity on space and time, it was a concept so mind-bending that years would pass before most physicists could accept it.

As soldiers died by droves at the front line and Germans at home began to succumb to epidemic and starvation under the British blockade, Einstein used his position to deride what he saw as the German "religion of power." "Honor your master Jesus Christ, not only with words and song, but above all by your deeds," he exhorted in a pacifist diatribe in 1915, unabashedly distinguishing himself as a Jew. If not by upbringing, Einstein was becoming a Jew by choice. And, unlike many German Jews inspired by the national mobilization, he held no hope that the heat of Jews' devotion to the Fatherland would at last melt their country's anti-Semitism.

One of the truest of these true believers was Einstein's friend and colleague Fritz Haber, a Jewish convert to Christianity and an eminent chemist eleven years his senior. Haber had earned his nation's gratitude by capturing nitrogen from the air, a process crucial to both farming and warfare. During World War I, he ingratiated himself further by developing the devastating green clouds of chlorine gas first released at the Battle of Ypres in 1915.

"Fritz Haber believed that if he converted to Christianity and wore a monocle, his Jewish heritage would disappear and he would become a good German," says Walter Isaacson. "The rise of anti-Semitism made people like Haber try all the harder to distance themselves from their Jewish background and to assimilate. It had an equal and opposite reaction in Einstein.

"When Haber was trying to conform by being the 'good German,'" Isaacson adds, "Einstein was willing to be an outsider and the proud Jew." Though they were close friends (indeed, Haber acted as go-between for Einstein and Maric), Einstein "was always brutal about Haber's pretensions," writes Thomas Levenson in *Einstein in Berlin*, mocking him as "that pathetic creature, the baptized Jewish privy councilor."

. . .

ON THE WEST AFRICAN island of Principe on May 29, 1919, Arthur Eddington stood in the rain adjusting the lenses of his telescopic camera, allowing himself just a few anxious glances skyward. Eddington, a quiet but droll professor of astronomy at Cambridge, was one of the only people outside Germany who believed in general relativity and one of the few in the world who claimed to understand it. On this day, if only the skies would clear, he intended to prove its merit.

The rain let up and he took a series of blurry photos of distant stars during the seven-minute eclipse that followed. While it would take six months to confirm, the data demonstrated that Einstein was right: light bends with gravity. Already esteemed in Germany, that November Einstein became a household name the world over, "the greatest Jew since Jesus," as one British scientist proclaimed.

In Berlin, he began to enjoy the pleasures of success. Löwenthal, elevated from paramour to legitimate hausfrau, liked to entertain in their tidy home outfitted with fine, heavy furniture and new carpets. Einstein came to count on the amenities of regular meals and nicely laundered clothing while he sought a little something on the side. It's hard to know whether his wife felt the sting more keenly when he kept his affairs secret or when, as was often the case, he conducted them openly.

Still, the bourgeois comforts of a famous man didn't blind Einstein to post-war Germany's renewed anti-Semitism. He coyly alluded to it in a "new relativity theory" based on the phenomenon of his renown: "Today in Germany, I am called a German man of science, and in England I am represented as a Swiss Jew...If I come to be represented as a bête noire, the descriptions will be reversed, and I shall become a Swiss Jew for the Germans and a German man of science for the English."

Einstein could joke, but the threat was real. Economic privations imposed by the Versailles reparations were even harsher than those of the war and Germany's economy was spiraling into collapse. "The hyperinflation was a gift to Adolf Hitler," who was just beginning to attract "local notoriety" as a mesmerizing, spit-spraying orator, writes Levenson. Einstein, he says, "recognized quickly that Hitler was not just another scummy politician but a qualitatively different kind of threat to Jews and to civilization."

Nowhere was resurgent anti-Semitism more obvious than in Germany's response to the arrival of the *Ostjuden*, the Eastern European Orthodox in their black caftans whom Einstein had come across in Prague. Destitute, fleeing pogroms, the war and the Russian Revolution, they poured into Berlin by the tens of thousands. German authorities addressed their plight by deporting them and detaining many in brutal prison camps. Even the Jews of Germany spurned them.

By contrast, Einstein joined lobbying committees, wrote editorials and played his violin in fundraising concerts for them. He saw how pointless (if not heartless) it was for western Jews to try to separate themselves from their cousins. To fellow Germans, he knew, this self-conscious divide constituted a distinction without a difference—his lone point of agreement, perhaps, with Hitler. As he would relate to a Purim dinner audience in 1935, "There are no German Jews; there are no Russian Jews; there are no American Jews. Their only difference is their daily language. There are in fact only Jews."

· · ·

IT WAS HOT THE NIGHT of August 24, 1920, when Einstein and Walther Nernst, his friend and colleague, strode through a raucous, shouting crowd gathered in front of Berlin's Philharmonic Hall. They managed to edge their way in without incident, despite the anti-Semitic literature being hawked at the door and the swastikas pasted everywhere. On offer inside was a lecture on relativity by the Working Group of German Scientists for the Preservation of Pure Science—"pure," in this case, meaning 19th-century Newtonian, and "German" meaning Aryan.

In other words, it was a "cockfight," according to Einstein who sat through it calmly, laughing and clapping his hands with relish at the most outlandish bits while various speakers called him a publicity hound and derided his theories as both wrong and stolen to boot. For Einstein, the rally's more chilling indication, given its presenters' second-rate scientific status, was that its organizers had found a previously respectable ally in Nobel Laureate Philipp Lenard, whose observations formed the basis of some of Einstein's own work. As the founder of a new "Anti-Relativity League," Lenard gave an establishment imprimatur to the accusations of "Jewish science" flying around Berlin. "Science," he pronounced, "like every other human product, is racial and conditioned by blood."

Beyond the academy, the attacks were even blunter, as Denis Brian described: "Einstein's less-articulate opponents waited outside his home or office…to greet him with obscenities, or crammed his mailbox with threats. At one of his Berlin lectures, a right-wing student shouted, 'I'm going to cut the throat of that dirty Jew!'"

For most of Berlin, shortages and breakdowns had become the norm (the Einsteins' apartment elevator no longer worked) and fatal street riots were growing commonplace as nationalists brawled with leftist revolutionaries. Even before Hitler gave form to their fascism, right-wing assassins had begun targeting prominent Communists, Jewish and otherwise, while Jews in the political center debated whether to play a role in Germany's shaky post-war democracy.

When Jewish industrial magnate Walter Rathenau was offered the post of foreign minister in 1922, Einstein allied himself with dedicated assimilationists in advising him against taking the job. "Einstein just had an instinct that, right after the loss in World War I and a treaty that others found humiliating, to have a Jewish foreign minister like Rathenau implementing the peace would cause resentment," Isaacson says. "It's hard to argue with him, since Rathenau was indeed assassinated." Shortly after, the Berlin police informed Einstein that his name, too, appeared on hit lists.

Einstein wisely began accepting invitations to lecture and teach abroad, commencing a decade of travel that would take him and his wife to many of Europe's major cities, as well as to Asia and the Americas. As refuge from the furies of Berlin, they also began vacationing in a nearby lake district. In 1929, they bought land there by a stand of trees overlooking the village of Caputh and hired young Jewish architect Konrad Wachsmann to build a modest vacation home on it in the spare style of the European Arts and Crafts movement. By September, they stood on its completed terrace, looking down past two tall pines and a little footpath to the serene surface of Lake Havel.

They entertained often in Caputh, but Einstein's happiest hours there were spent on barefoot hikes and sailing, usually alone, often for hours. For his 50th birthday in March that year, wealthy friends had given him a pretty wooden boat. He named it *Tümmler*, a Yiddish word with two meanings: "life of the party" and "agitator."

. . .

As 8,000 NEW YORKERS pushed their way into the 69th Regiment Armory on April 12, 1921, another 3,000 jammed the sidewalks outside. Zionist leader Chaim Weizmann, a British chemist and Russian emigré, soberly regaled the audience inside about marsh reclamation and bold pioneers in the new Jewish homeland.

Weizmann may have been the prime mover behind the 1917 Balfour Declaration that opened Palestine to Jewish settlement, but he had cleverly recruited the world's most famous Jew to accompany him on his barnstorming trip through New York, New Jersey, Illinois, Massachusetts, Ohio and Washington, DC. He knew that tens of thousands of American Jews in their Shabbat best might not turn out for him but would go crazy for Dr. Einstein. The scientist's every arrival inspired parades and drew crowds willing to empty their purses. Even the press whipped itself into a froth of reporting on the Zionist mission and what Einstein ate for breakfast.

While Weizmann lectured on, Einstein smiled vaguely from the dais. He wasn't scheduled to speak, but the audience's demanding roar filled the cavernous, steel-beamed hall. Reluctantly, he stepped to the podium. "Your leader, Dr. Weizmann, has spoken…Follow him and you will do well. That is all I have to say."

The speech was three sentences in all. Weizmann must have breathed a sigh of relief as he reflected on the warning imparted by a friend before their trip: "Please be careful with Einstein. [He] often says things out of naiveté which are unwelcome to us."

Einstein, who would later say he "discovered the Jewish people" in the American throngs, had actually surprised Weizmann by accepting the invitation to America. The Zionists knew Einstein to be anything but an "organization man"—he never officially joined a Zionist group—and realized that Jewish dreams of nationhood ran against his one-world bias. But the *Ostjuden* still milling hopelessly in Berlin's slums, and the slurs of Lenard and his ilk must have been fresh in Einstein's mind when the call came.

Since the tour required missing a prestigious international meeting of physicists, he tried to explain the choice to Maurice Solovine, a friend from his Zurich days. "I am not at all eager to go to America," he wrote, "but am doing it only in the interests of the Zionists who must beg for dollars to build educational institutions in Jerusalem and for whom I act as high priest and decoy."

Their tour raised nearly a million dollars, enough to begin construction of a medical campus for Hebrew University. Whether it was situated in a state, homeland or Mandate, Einstein felt as keenly as any Jew the need for a Jewish center of learning in Palestine. "I know of no public event," he told *The New York Times*, "that has given me such pleasure as the proposal to establish a Hebrew University in Jerusalem. The traditional respect for knowledge that Jews have maintained intact through many centuries of severe hardship has made it particularly painful for us to see so many talented sons of the Jewish people cut off from higher education."

Zionism may have offended his Universalist sensibilities, but it emerged for Einstein between the world wars as "a nationalism that does not strive for power but for dignity and recovery"— the single rallying cause that could strengthen his beleaguered people. He concluded that "the only way to cope with anti-Semitism [was] to restore a communal solidarity, a communal pride among the Jews," according to Hebrew University's Gutfreund.

Characteristically, Einstein saw this pride as a benefit not strictly for Jews but rather, through their elevation and development, for all people. A safe and settled Jewry, he reasoned, free to develop its human potential, could draw on ethical heritage and the "genius of their prophets" to exert a healthy moral leadership in the world while sharing its expertise in medicine and, of course, science.

Rather than the theocratic state sought by many, he thought the way to achieve Jewish fulfillment in Palestine was through a "national home" under a Jewish-Arab or even international government entity. As late as 1938, he told an audience of New York Zionists, "I should much rather see a reasonable agreement with the Arabs based on living together in peace than the creation of a Jewish state." Einstein cautioned repeatedly against the "inner damage" that the Jewish people would sustain as result of the "narrow nationalism" that accompanies statehood.

Einstein had the chance to see his communal ideals in action in 1923. Spooked by the death of Rathenau the previous year, he accepted a standing invitation to travel for several months in Asia, followed by a visit to Palestine. On his 12-day tour, Einstein stopped in at schools and planted a tree. He played chamber music with the attorney general and his sisters, and Tel Aviv named him its first honorary citizen. Amid these secular engagements also came an invitation that testified to Einstein's importance in every corner of Jewry. It came from Rav Abraham Kook, the Lithuanian-born chief rabbi of Palestine. The eminent rabbi and Einstein met in Jerusalem, where they were said to have discussed Kabbalah among other subjects.

"The brothers of our race in Palestine charmed me as farmers, workers and citizens," he wrote to Solovine. Yet the tour was by no means a second conversion. With his usual bluntness and despite his support of the *Ostjuden*, he dismissed daveners at the Western Wall in his diary as "dull-witted clansmen of our tribe...A pathetic sight of men with a past but without a future."

Einstein nevertheless inaugurated a more hopeful Israelite future when he delivered Hebrew University's first scientific lecture from the front of a British police hall on Mount Scopus. "Professor Einstein," went the introduction, "please rise to the podium that has been waiting for you two thousand years." Einstein opened with a few halting sentences in Hebrew before reverting to French for the body of his talk. He could have spoken Swahili and still projected his message: In his voice, as Gutfreund, the institution's later president would write, Einstein's audience heard "the birth song of the long-anticipated Jewish university."

• • •

A DRIZZLE WAS FALLING on the late summer day in 1932 that American education reformer Abraham Flexner arrived in Caputh. The Kentucky-born Flexner had bulked up against the weather, so he was surprised to find Einstein relaxing on the porch in summer flannels, apparently oblivious to the cold.

Ensconced in Caputh's airy comforts, Einstein seemed likewise oblivious to the political chill in Berlin: students protesting against sharing their campuses with Jews; Nazi toughs shouting slogans and threats in train corridors; and Hitler's growing clout in the Reichstag. Through an intermediary, the army's commander-in-chief had sent a warning that Einstein's life was no longer safe. Even in his haven, a maid reported that Caputh's baker had begun muttering darkly about the Jew on the hill.

Flexner had come to offer Einstein a way out, a yellow brick road to America. This was their third meeting to discuss the nascent Institute for Advanced Study, an academic Valhalla intended to seed American scholarship. Like the Kaiser Institute representatives who drew Einstein from Zurich back in 1913, Flexner knew Einstein's assent could ensure his project's success. Also like them, he dangled the offer of a prestigious and amply compensated post in a rarefied academic community.

Still, Einstein hated to leave his refuge. It took a few weeks of negotiations and importuning but he eventually agreed to reside at the Institute five months each year, reserving the right to return to Caputh and his comfortable *Tümmler* life if Hitler faded from the picture. In December, he and Löwenthal rode the train to Caputh to close up their cottage. Their departure from Germany would be temporary, according to every official and public statement, and yet, as they closed the door on their familiar rooms and the ghosts of entertainments past, Einstein told his wife to take a good look around, for she might never see the house again. He was right.

Again an immigrant, again a guest, again a face in the prospect of war, Einstein felt the need to speak out in America. This time, however, the onetime pacifist condemned the failure to start a war against the existential threat in Europe. "I cannot understand the passive response of the whole civilized world to this modern barbarism," he cried in a 1933 interview. "Does the world not see that Hitler is aiming at war?" And did America's Jews not see that he was targeting their coreligionists first of all?

In contrast to Berlin of 1914, however, this time Einstein could act. Having settled in Princeton permanently in 1933 and helped transform Flexner's Institute into an exemplar of American research, he was also shaping it into a refuge and hub for Europe's persecuted scholars. He could have done otherwise, succumbing to the easy routines of his suburban hideaway. Yet this very contentment spurred him to action. "I am," he confessed in a letter to the queen of Belgium, a longtime friend, "almost ashamed to be living in such a place while all the rest struggle and suffer."

No storm troopers threatened to interrupt his twice-daily strolls along Princeton's quiet leafy streets to the Institute's borrowed space at Princeton University. In fact, locals went to great lengths to protect the professor's privacy. To visitors—both expected and not—who streamed through the little wrought-iron gate and up to the front porch of the narrow clapboard house he and Löwenthal bought at 112 Mercer Street, Einstein proved a shy but genial host. Boys from the Princeton Country Day School, after struggling fruitlessly over a math set, once brought it to Einstein for help, and he seldom rebuffed strangers who approached him on the street with questions or greetings. Löwenthal died in 1936, but Einstein remained in the house in the company of her daughter Margot, his devoted secretary Helen Dukas and, after 1939, his sister.

As "Professor Einstein," he still filled his hours with calculations and jottings related to physics, but these were dormant years for theoretical breakthroughs. Many younger colleagues, in fact, suspected the old man was washed up, chasing a pipe dream with his single-minded focus on finding a "unified field theory" that would unite the laws of physics under a single model. ("How ironic," physicist Lee Smolin wrote in *My Einstein* in 2006, "that now the Institute is filled with young people playing with unified field theories.")

As "Citizen Einstein," however, he was anything but dormant, almost biblical—a whirlwind and scourge to the complacent, most notably on behalf of his endangered people. Even while still in Europe, during a final 1933 stay in Belgium, Löwenthal had complained that the Einsteins' temporary home had turned into "an asylum for the unfortunate, invaded from morning to night by people who need help." In the States, he scoured the Institute and other universities to find temporary sinecures for Jewish academics trapped in Europe. He proposed names of prominent scientists, artists and thinkers for U.S. emergency visas, and he met with President Franklin Roosevelt at the White House in 1934 to plead for more of them. In 1939, fellow immigré physicists asked him to petition Roosevelt again— this time for research toward a nuclear weapon, so the Germans wouldn't develop one first. Perhaps with Haber's gas clouds in mind, he obliged.

Einstein worked feverishly to rescue kin, friends, kin of friends and even strangers from the maw of Hitler's Germany. He personally vouched for dozens, establishing in their names as many $2,000 bank accounts (required by immigration authorities) as he could afford. When tapped out, he beseeched friends and colleagues to put up funds, guaranteeing the deposits himself. In addition to university professors, he helped bring over non-academics like Wachsmann, his Caputh architect, and future *Life* magazine photographer Philip Halsmann. In 1941, he took in theoretical physicist Fritz Reiche, one of the last Jewish scientists to slip out of Nazi Germany.

Einstein personally petitioned for so many refugees that, by the end of 1930s, his once influential signature at the bottom of an affidavit had ceased to carry weight. Beyond the visa race, he toured the fundraising circuit for Zionist institutions, refugee groups and other Jewish causes. He graced daises at dinners, fiddled in benefit concerts and donated his books and manuscripts for auction.

· · ·

BY THE TIME HE APPROACHED the front stoop of Marion Epstein's modest stucco house in downtown Princeton, the war was over and Einstein's worst fears about Europe had been realized. Epstein played it cool when he knocked, ushering Einstein into her small living room with no more fuss than she made over the dozen or so others arriving that evening to plan the Princeton's United Jewish Appeal's spring fundraising dinner at the Nassau Tavern.

Epstein, now 91, did give the honorary chairman the best seat, "a big, comfortable armchair," she recalls. There Einstein sat, quietly balancing his cake and teacup on his knees, while the committee made schedules and drafted the invitation.

One of the best ways to meet the famous Albert Einstein in the 1940s was to join the Princeton UJA. "He was always willing to give his name," Epstein recalls matter-of-factly. "He was quiet, friendly, simple. There was no pride of fame." Epstein, a UJA board member, had also helped organize Sunday socials for Jewish officer candidates housed at the university during the war. "Einstein came to one of those," she recalls. "One of the women brought her teacup from home and made sure he drank from it!"

Einstein was more in demand than ever for causes he cared about, scientific and political, Jewish and secular. "What the individual can do," he once explained, "is give a fine example, and have the courage to firmly uphold ethical convictions in a society of cynics." Einstein upheld his convictions by denouncing both Senator Joseph McCarthy and Joseph Stalin at the height of their powers; he championed the rights of African Americans in the heyday of Jim Crow (befriending Paul Robeson and hosting Marian Anderson more than once at his house when the Nassau Tavern turned her away); and he showed no patience for materialism and pomp. For Jews, he opined in a 1932 essay, "'serving God' meant 'serving the living.' The best of the Jewish people, especially the Prophets and Jesus, contended tirelessly for this."

And Einstein contended tirelessly for the Jews, seeming, like some quantum spark, to be in several places at once. As on his 1921 junket with Weizmann, the interests of Jewish institutions of higher learning lay close to his heart. The only difference is that they were now in the United States as well as Israel. In 1946, he let organizers of what would become Brandeis University name their start-up foundation the "Albert Einstein Foundation for Higher Learning, Inc." In 1948, New York's Yeshiva University asked for his name on the Albert Einstein School of Medicine, which opened the year he died. For Hebrew University, which had named its school of mathematics for him, Einstein ceaselessly sought funds and favors. And he served on an advisory committee for an institute in Rehovot later named for his friend Weizmann, to which he donated a trove of personal papers in 1946 and which, in 1980, opened the Albert Einstein Center for Theoretical Physics.

Nevertheless, where Palestine's politics were concerned, Zionists still had reason to fear unwelcome statements from their "high priest and decoy." As late as 1946, Einstein would still testify against Jewish governance to the Anglo-American Committee of Inquiry on Palestine. But as in Germany, where racism had helped Einstein forge his Jewish identity, world events now persuaded him of the need for a Jewish state.

"It was a gradual process," Gutfreund says of Einstein's change of heart. "There was a disappointment in the policies of the British Mandate authorities; there was a disappointment of the rejection by the Arab League of all his attempts at overtures to understanding; and then there was the realization that the whole enterprise might be lost, be destroyed," without outside support.

Reconciling this support with his innate pacifism would always be a struggle. In *Tea With Einstein*, author William Frankel said that Einstein railed against Jewish guerilla warfare under the British in 1946. "Einstein was passionate in his denunciation of the Irgun and the Stern Gang," Frankel wrote, "even though he conceded that its militant activities could possibly advance the creation of the Jewish state which was, in his opinion, both desirable and inevitable."

When President Harry Truman recognized Israel in May 1948, Einstein declared it "the fulfillment of our dreams." Perceiving its vulnerability after independence, he again set aside his pacifism in the name of human preservation. "No one respects or bothers about those who do not fight for their rights," a changed Einstein wrote to his cousin in Uruguay. As planned, the cousin auctioned off Einstein's letter, raising $5,000 to buy arms for the Haganah.

Even as a critic of Israel, Einstein's dedication to his people guaranteed his great stature among world Jewry. No incident better proved that point than what transpired after the death of Israel's first president, Chaim Weizmann, in November 1952. Inside of a week, readers of Israel's *Maariv* newspaper had proposed the 73-year-old Einstein, "the greatest Jew alive," to succeed him. When a telegram arrived requesting an audience for Israeli Ambassador Abba Eban at 112 Mercer, Einstein was alarmed. How to let the Israelis down gently? he wondered.

Einstein telephoned Eban to head him off but the diplomat insisted on at least sending over a formal letter of invitation. Einstein met Eban's emissary with a letter of his own, explaining that a position like Israel's presidency required etiquette and interpersonal finesse—traits that he, rightly, claimed to lack. While publicly disappointed, his petitioners were privately relieved by the turndown: "Tell me what to do if he accepts," Prime Minister Ben-Gurion had urged an aide. "If he does, we are in for trouble!"

Einstein took pains over his "rejection letter" to the people of Israel. "My relationship to the Jewish people has become my strongest human bond," he wrote, "ever since I became fully aware of our precarious situation among the nations of the world."

. . .

ON THE MORNING OF April 17, 1955 Albert Einstein lay in bed at Princeton Hospital. An aortic aneurysm he had known about for years was rupturing and he expected to die soon, but the 75-year-old felt well enough this day to wield a pencil. He had work to do on his field theory and yet another mission to benefit Jews and Israel. Just days before, he had invited Ambassador Eban to his home to offer a modest proposal: Would the Israelis like him to record a national radio address on Israel's behalf? "I must challenge the conscience of the world," he told Eban, and "boldly criticize the world powers for their attitude to Israel." The speech was planned to coincide with Israeli Independence Day at the end of the month.

Einstein died early the next morning. Left by his bedside were "12 pages of tightly written equations," as Isaacson described, and preliminary notes for the speech that began: "I speak to you today not as an American citizen and not as a Jew, but as a human being."

By evening, Einstein's body had been cremated with just 12 mourners on hand. In keeping with the way he had lived, Einstein's funeral was absent of ritual. Someone recited a bit of Goethe but, at his request, no prayers were said. Nor did Einstein wish to leave behind a memorial or gravesite. His ashes were strewn over the nearby Delaware River.

Though Einstein left the world without a physical monument to his existence, it can be said that he gave literally his all to the Jewish people. In life, he liberally lent his prestige and name and, as in the case of the UJA and the Princeton students, his presence. After death, Einstein found a way to continue giving. He left orders in his will for a trust to be formed containing "all of my manuscripts, copyrights, publication rights" and, most significantly in hindsight, all other rights. The trust's income was designated for his dependents—Dukas and his stepdaughter Margot—as long as they lived. After that, its contents and income reverted to Hebrew University.

To a degree that Einstein may never have imagined, that gift has kept on giving. Scholars and the public enjoy free access to his vast writings and correspondence (including thousands of pages online), but those who would use Einstein's name and image for commercial ends must pay for the privilege. Every Einstein T-shirt or poster, each Baby Einstein toy, the many Apple "Think Different" ads, all earn money for Einstein's beloved institute of Jewish learning.

For the rest of the Jewish people, he left a less tangible but equally valuable legacy: a clearly marked ethical trail for those courageous enough to follow it. With relativity, Einstein paved new roads for scientists. With his own life, he pioneered new ways to live as a Jew. ෯

2

IN CHAMBERS WITH
RUTH BADER GINSBURG

Abigail Pogrebin • *January/February 2006*

JUSTICE RUTH BADER GINSBURG has a run in her stocking, which, I must admit, puts me at ease. It's my first time in a U.S. Supreme Court Justice's chambers—even that word, "chambers," conveys hushed, erudite activity—and it's strangely comforting to see that this tiny woman with the giant intellect gets runs in her hose like the rest of us. "Why don't we just sit here," she gestures to a couch in her sitting area.

Ginsburg, often described as small and soft-spoken, appears almost miniaturized in her sizable office space, formerly occupied by the late Thurgood Marshall. Dressed all in black—slacks, blouse, stockings, sandals, a shawl draped around her shoulders—she looks like a frail Spanish widow rather than one of the nine most powerful jurists in the land.

But it's clear that despite her petite frame, small voice, and a battle with colon cancer, Ginsburg—age seventy at the time we are meeting, the second woman on the bench in the court's history and its first Jewish member since Abe Fortas—is formidable. She tells one story that illustrates her intrepid style: "My first year here, the court clerk, who is just a very fine fellow, came to me and said, 'Every year we get letters from Orthodox Jews who would like to have a Supreme Court membership certificate that doesn't say 'In the year of our Lord.' [She's referring to the certificate lawyers receive when they become members of the Supreme Court bar.] So I said, 'I agree; if they don't want that, they shouldn't have it.'

"So I checked to see what the federal courts and circuit courts were doing and discovered, to my horror, that in my thirteen years on the DC circuit, the membership certificate has always said, 'In the year of our Lord.' So I spoke to the chief judges of all the circuits, and some of them had already made the change, others were glad to make the change. Then I came to my Chief and said, 'All the other circuits give people a choice.'" Her "Chief," William Rehnquist, recommended she raise the issue "in conference" with her fellow justices, which she did. "I won't tell you the name of this particular colleague," she says, "but when I brought this up and thought it would be a no-brainer, one of my colleagues said, 'The year of our Lord was good enough for Brandeis, it was good enough for Cardozo, it was good enough—'and I said, 'Stop. It's not good enough for Ginsburg.'"

Significant laws have been changed over the last few decades because the status quo wasn't "good enough for Ginsburg." She is known as a pioneer in the field of antidiscrimination law, a founder of the Women's Rights Project of the American Civil Liberties Union, the first female tenured professor at Columbia University Law School, and the lawyer who argued six women's rights cases before the Supreme Court and won five of them.

She abandoned traditional Judaism because it wasn't "good enough for Ginsburg" either. Its exclusion of women from meaningful rituals was painfully brought home to her at age seventeen, when her mother, Celia Bader, succumbed to cancer a day before Ruth's high school graduation. "When my mother died, the house was filled with women; but only men could participate in the minyan [the quorum required for public prayers]."

It didn't matter that the young Ruth had worked hard to be confirmed at Brooklyn's East Midwood Jewish Center—"I was one of the few people who took it seriously," she remarks—or that at thirteen, she'd been the "camp rabbi" at a Jewish summer program. Having a Jewish education counted for nothing at one of the most important moments in her life. "That time was not a good one for me in terms of organized religion," she says with typical understatement. I ask her to expand on how Judaism made her feel secondary. "It had something to do with being a girl. I wasn't trained to be a yeshiva *bucher*."

Later, she was also turned off by the class system in her family synagogue. "This is something I'll tell you and you know it exists: In many temples, where you sit depends on how much money you give to the shul. And my parents went to the synagogue, Temple Beth El in Belle Harbor, Long Island—it's right next to Rockaway. When my mother died and my father's [furrier] business went down the drain, he was no longer able to contribute to the temple. And so their tickets for the High Holy Days were now in the annex, not in the main temple, although they had been members since the year they married. And I just—that whole episode was not pleasing to me at all."

Neither was the time when she tried to enroll her son, James, in Sunday school at Temple Emanu-El on Fifth Avenue in New York City. "The rabbi told me to fill out the application for membership 'as though I were my husband,'" she recalls with indignation. "I said, 'Well I haven't consulted him; I don't know if he wants to be a member of Temple Emanu-El.'"

"The idea was, as a woman, if you were not single, widowed, or divorced, you could not be a member. If you were married, then your husband was the member. I was still teaching at Rutgers—it was 1972. And I remember how annoyed I was. Still, I wanted James to have something of a Jewish education. So I said, 'I will make a contribution to the temple that is equivalent to the membership, if you will allow my child to attend Sunday school.'" I ask her if these bouts with sexism were what kept her from embracing Jewish observance. Again she's not expansive. "Yes," she answers softly. "Yes."

Despite giving up synagogue attendance, Sabbath candle-lighting, and fasting on Yom Kippur, Ginsburg did go to her husband's parents' home for Passovers. "That was always a great time for the children," she says. "I think even more for my children than it was for me." Her husband, Martin Ginsburg, a respected tax lawyer and an accomplished cook, occasionally dabbled in Jewish ethnic cuisine. "In his very early days he made his mother's chopped liver," she says with a smile.

Her children were bored with Sunday school, and she didn't urge them to stick it out. "James was not bar mitzvahed," she says of her younger son, "and that was his choice. He didn't want to do the studying. We were living in California at that time—we were at Stanford [where she was a Fellow at the Center for Advanced Study in the Behavioral Sciences]. James did not like the Sunday school there, and I didn't want to have one more issue in his life." Her daughter, Jane, ducked Sunday school more cannily. "She made a deal with us." Ginsburg smiles. "We were then going to a much nicer Sunday school at Shaaray Tefila on East 79th Street in New York City, but Jane didn't like it very much. She is ten and a half years older than her brother. One Sunday morning, when he was an infant, I overslept; she took care of him and didn't go to Sunday school. And I was so glad that she did such a good job. So she said that she would make a deal with us: If she didn't have to go to Sunday school anymore, she would take care of James every Sunday morning. That was an offer I could hardly refuse. So that's when she stopped.

"But Jane became very Jewish again when she married a Catholic boy," Ginsburg continues. "First, she wanted to have a rabbi reassure her that even if her children were baptized—which they were because it was important to my son-in-law's Italian-Catholic mother—that it could still be a Jewish baby. And I thought that would be easy." Ginsburg shakes her neatly chignoned head. "But it was very, very hard to find a rabbi who would say that. Ab [Abner] Mikva was my chief judge on the DC Circuit Court. His daughter is a rabbi and she said, 'No, I won't tell her that.'"

I remark that this must have been very upsetting. "Yes," Ginsburg says with a nod, "but I said to Jane, 'This woman [the Italian-Catholic mother-in-law] is thinking that if her grandchild isn't baptized, this child's soul will never go to heaven. So it's just to put her at ease.'"

Did it matter to Justice Ginsburg that her children marry Jews? "No. Jane is married to a very fine man who is perfect for her. And she had anticipated all kinds of difficulties that didn't arise. There was a question of Sunday school and I said, 'Wait till George—my son-in-law—finds the church that he is going to enroll Paul and Clara in.' And he never did—to this day he hasn't. My granddaughter, who will be thirteen in October, is this summer—for the second time—going to a Hadassah-run camp on the French side of Lake Geneva. So now she knows more about Judaism than I have forgotten."

Ginsburg seems comforted by a sense that her grandchildren know what's at the heart of their birthright. "I think they have enough of an understanding that, when you are a Jew, the world will look at you that way; and this is a heritage that you can be very proud of. That this small band of people has survived such perils over the centuries. And that the Jews love learning, they're the people of the book. So it's a heritage to be proud of. And then, too, it's something that you can't escape because the world won't let you; so it's a good thing that you can be proud of it."

So what does it mean to be Jewish without rituals? "Think of how many prominent people in different fields identify themselves proudly as Jews but don't take part in the rituals," Ginsburg replies. She adds that even without observance, being Jewish still matters greatly to her. "I'll show you one symbol of that which is here"—she gets up—"if you come." We walk across her office, which is surprisingly ordinary—no dark paneled walls, inlaid desks, or library lamps. It looks more like a civil service office with gray carpeting, tan puffy leather chairs, and a round glass table (with a stuffed Jiminy Cricket doll sitting on top). The only clue to Ginsburg's personality is the profusion of family photos propped on her bookshelves—pictures of her son, James, who produces classical music recordings from Chicago; daughter, Jane, who teaches literary and artistic property law at Columbia; the two grandchildren; and of course, the requisite Ginsburg-with-presidents series—Carter, Clinton, Bush Sr., George W.

She guides me to her main office door, where a gold mezuzah is nailed prominently to its frame. "At Christmas around here, every door has a wreath," she explains. "I received this mezuzah from the Shulamith School for Girls in Brooklyn, and it's a way of saying, 'This is my space, and please don't put a wreath on this door.'"

Her barometer for religious insensitivity rises not just around Christmas time, but at the beginning of each court term. "Before every session, there's a Red Mass [in a Catholic church]," she says. "And the justices get invitations from the cardinal to attend. And not all—but a good number—of the justices show up every year. I went one year and I will never go again, because this sermon was outrageously anti-abortion. Even the Scalias—although they're very much of that persuasion—were embarrassed for me." (She and Justice Antonin Scalia are close friends who have celebrated many New Year's Eves together, despite their profound ideological differences.)

Clearly, Ginsburg takes symbolism seriously. Though others might view it as nitpicking, she's always deemed it worth her effort and prestige to challenge small inequities, in addition to working toward large-scale reform. Thus, the changed language in the lawyer's certificate, the jettisoned wreaths, the boycotted Red Mass, and most recently the blacked-out First Monday in October: "We are not sitting on the first Monday in October this year and we will not sit on any first Monday that coincides with Yom Kippur," she says proudly. "Now, this is the first year that is happening. The first time Yom Kippur came up, it was an ad hoc decision—we were not going to sit that Monday. But now, this is the way it's going to be from now on." Having her comrade Jew on the court, Stephen Breyer, lobbying alongside her was crucial, she says. "In this great Yom Kippur controversy, it helped very much that there were two of us."

Her final show-and-tell items are framed, calligraphic renderings of the Hebrew command from Deuteronomy: "Tzcdck, Tzcdck, *tirdorf* — "Justice, Justice shalt thou pursue." Ginsburg says it was her mother who put Jewish tradition in the context more of doing justice than of observance. "My mother had mixed memories of her Judaism because her father was ultra-Orthodox; she remembers her eldest brother worked very hard to ride a bicycle and then his father caught him riding on the Sabbath and broke it to pieces. So that type of fanatic observance my mother did not appreciate. On the other hand, she has very pleasant memories of the Sabbath and the smell of the bread; and it was the one day that her mother wasn't working—wasn't cooking all the time."

Ginsburg's mother pushed her daughter hard to succeed. "My mother told me to be independent. She thought that meant I'd be a high school history teacher." Does Ginsburg consider that emphasis on achievement to be Jewish? "Yes," she answers definitively. "I loved my mother dearly and she was constantly supporting my reading, sometimes pushing me to do things that I didn't really care about, like math. And she cared in a way that other mothers didn't. Our neighborhood was divided three ways—it was Italian, Irish, and Jewish in equal parts. And the Jewish parents were much more concerned about how their children were doing in school."

• • •

WHEN GINSBURG STOOD AT President Clinton's side during her nomination ceremony in 1993, she discussed the hurdles she faced at the start of her law career. "I had three strikes against me," she recalled. "I was Jewish, I was a woman, and I was a mother. So if a door would have been open a crack in either of the first two cases, the third one was too much." One of her first jobs—between college and law school—was in a Social Security office working for a man who'd never met a Jew before. "He wasn't entirely sure I wasn't hiding horns somewhere in my head," she says with a half smile.

In her first year at Cornell, she says, the anti-Semitism was visible but unspoken. "In the dormitory, all of the girls on both sides were Jewish," she recalls. "That didn't happen by chance. The houses were arranged so that we would not contaminate all the others. We were contained." She adds that this made for lasting bonds. "We are friends to this day—it was a wonderful group of people."

I ask if the "outsiderness" she felt over the years proved to be a motivating force. "Oh, it certainly is," she replies without her usual hesitation. "You've got to be sure you were better than anyone else."

So I ask the obvious question, "Does being Jewish affect the way you approach cases on the Court?"—expecting her to wave it off with some boilerplate version of 'Justices can't let personal experience color their judgment.' Instead, her answer is more nuanced. "I don't think that I approach cases in a particular way because I am Jewish any more than I do because I'm a woman. I have certain sensitivities for both. You know the old expression, 'Is it good for the Jews?' For example, a lot of people want to have crosses in front of their town hall or whatever. They say, 'It doesn't hurt anybody.' We had one case where I was in dissent—it was about a cross in front of the statehouse in Ohio. And to me, the photograph of that statehouse told the whole story of the case: Here is the Capitol in Columbus, and here is this giant cross. And what is the perception of a Jewish child who is passing by the Capitol? It's certainly that this is a Christian country. A person's reaction could be: 'There's something wrong with me.' It's not a symbol that includes you."

The theme of exclusion runs through so many of her stories: the sting of being sidelined, legal cases about people who are made to feel unwelcome. A sad irony occurs to me, as she talks: As other institutions marginalized her for being a Jew, her religion made her feel left out because she was a woman and thus lost her early on. When I ask if she misses Judaism, there's a long pause. "I wish that I could have the feeling for it that I once did. I don't think I ever will." ✆

3

THE STORY OF SERGEY BRIN

Mark Malseed • *February/March 2007*

IT TAKES A BIT OF SEARCHING to find Sergey Brin's office at the Googleplex. Tucked away in a corner of Building #43 on this sprawling campus near the southern tip of San Francisco Bay, past rows of colorfully decorated cubicles and dorm-like meeting spaces, Office 211 has a nondescript exterior and sits far from the public eye. Although it requires several twists and turns to get there, his office is not protected—as you would expect for the co-founder of a $150-billion company—by a Russian nesting doll's worth of doors and gatekeepers.

Sergey, 33, shares the space with his Google co-founder, fellow Stanford Ph.D. dropout and billionaire pal, 34-year-old Larry Page, an arrangement that began eight years ago in the company's first humble headquarters in a Menlo Park, California garage. Since then, Google has grown from just another Silicon Valley startup into the world's largest media corporation; in fact, based on its recent stock price of $513 per share, Google, which has made searching the Web easy and even fun, is larger than Disney, General Motors and McDonald's combined. It achieved these lofty heights by revolutionizing how people surf the Internet: Before Sergey and Larry analyzed the links between web pages to deliver search results speedily based on relevance, looking up information on the Web was a shot in the dark.

Stepping through the sliding glass door into their office is like walking into a playroom for tech-savvy adults. A row of sleek flat-screen monitors lining one wall displays critical information: email, calendars, documents and, naturally, the Google search engine. Assorted green plants and an air purifier keep the oxygen flowing, while medicine balls provide appropriately kinetic seating. Upstairs, a private mezzanine with Astroturf carpeting and an electric massage chair afford Sergey and Larry a comfortable perch from which to entertain visitors and survey the carnival of innovation going on below. And there is ample space for walking around, which is absolutely essential for Sergey, who just can't seem to sit still.

Trim and boyishly handsome, with low sloping shoulders that give him a perpetually relaxed appearance, Sergey bounces around the Googleplex with apparently endless energy. He has dark hair, penetrating eyes and a puckish sense of humor that often catches people off guard. A typical workday finds him in jeans, sneakers and a fitted black T-shirt, though his casual manner belies a serious, even aggressive sense of purpose. This intensity emerges during weekly strategy meetings, where Sergey and Larry—who share the title of president—command the last word on approving new products, reviewing new hires and funding long-term research. Sergey also holds sway over the unscientific but all-important realms of people, policy and politics. Google's workers enjoy such family-friendly perks as three free meals a day, free home food delivery for new parents, designated private spaces for nursing mothers, and full on-site medical care, all of which recently led *Fortune* magazine to rank the company as the #1 place to work in the country.

The co-presidents share management duties with Eric Schmidt, a seasoned software executive whom they hired as chief executive officer in 2001 to oversee the day-to-day aspects of Google's business—in short, to be the "adult" in the playroom. But they have no intention of ceding control. Since day one, they have resisted outside meddling, preferring to do everything their own way, from opting to piece together computers on the cheap (and build a computer casing out of Lego blocks) to flouting Wall Street in an unconventional initial public offering.

Blazing one's own trail comes naturally to Sergey. The Moscow-born entrepreneur and his parents have been doing it their entire lives.

• • •

ON DECEMBER 16, 2005, 16 months after the company's high-flying initial stock auction, Google closed its biggest deal yet: a $1-billion advertising partnership with America Online, the popular Internet service provider.

That evening, by coincidence, I am meeting with Sergey's parents at their home in the suburbs of Washington, DC. Michael Brin, wearing a black fleece vest emblazoned with the multicolored Google logo, greets me in the driveway. I ask if he has heard the big news. "We spoke with Sergey earlier today and he didn't mention anything," he tells me. "He did say he was on his way home from yoga."

Michael, 59, a mathematics professor at the University of Maryland, and his wife, Eugenia, 58, a research scientist at NASA's Goddard Space Flight Center, are gracious and down-to-earth and still somewhat astonished by their son's success. "It's mind-boggling," marvels Genia, as family and friends call her. She speaks slowly, in a syrupy, Russian-accented English that quickens when she is competing with her husband. "It's hard to comprehend, really. He was a very capable child in math and computers, but we could have never imagined this." Michael, in his milder accent, adds with typical pragmatism, "Google has saved more time for more people than anything else in the world."

They sit me down at the dining room table, clearing off papers to make space for a spread of cheese and fruit. The room itself is simply decorated, even sparse; the only signs of wealth I can see anywhere are a big-screen TV in the living room and a Lexus in the driveway.

The Brins are a compact, young-looking couple; Michael is skeptical in demeanor with a precise manner of speaking, and Genia is soft and nurturing. Both have sincere, easygoing laughs. We talk for several hours, interrupted occasionally by Michael's cigarette breaks, for which he heads outside with the family dog, Toby. Smoking is a habit he brought with him from the Soviet Union in 1979, when he immigrated to the United States with his mother, Maya, Genia and Sergey, then six. (A second son, Sam, was born in 1987.)

One of Michael's stories particularly strikes me. In the summer of 1990, a few weeks before Sergey's 17th birthday, Michael led a group of gifted high school math students on a two-week exchange program to the Soviet Union. He decided to bring the family along, despite uneasiness about the welcome they could expect from Communist authorities. It would give them a chance to visit family members still living in Moscow, including Sergey's paternal grandfather, like Michael, a Ph.D. mathematician.

It didn't take long for Sergey, a precocious teenager about to enter college, to size up his former environs. The Soviet empire was crumbling and, in the drab, cinder-block landscape and people's stony mien of resignation, he could see first-hand the bleak future that would have been his. On the second day of the trip, while the group toured a sanitarium in the countryside near Moscow, Sergey took his father aside, looked him in the eye and said, "Thank you for taking us all out of Russia."

"There were only two occasions when my children were grateful to me," Michael says dryly, and I get the sense that he is completely serious. The other occasion, he says, involved Sergey's younger brother, Sam, and the repair of a broken toilet.

Genia, seated next to him, protests. "Misha, what are you talking about!?" she exclaims, as she often does when their memories differ or when she feels Michael is editorializing.

As Sergey recalls, the trip awakened his childhood fear of authority. His crisp tenor voice, tinged with a faint accent that is no longer identifiably Russian, came to me via satellite phone as he flew to Asia last November. Teenagers have their own way of transforming fear into defiance, Sergey reflects, remembering that his impulse on confronting Soviet oppression had been to throw pebbles at a police car. The two officers sitting inside got out of the car "quite upset" he says but, luckily, his parents were able to defuse the matter.

"My rebelliousness, I think, came out of being born in Moscow," Sergey says, adding, "I'd say this is something that followed me into adulthood."

. . .

AT A BAGEL SHOP ACROSS the street from the Maryland campus where he has taught dynamical systems and statistics for 25 years, Michael talks of the discrimination that drove him to take his family out of Russia. It's a bitter cold day in College Park, reminiscent of winter in Moscow. Over a lunch of soup and sandwiches, Michael explains how he was forced to abandon his dream of becoming an astronomer even before he reached college. Officially, anti-Semitism didn't exist in the U.S.S.R. but, in reality, Communist Party heads barred Jews from upper professional ranks by denying them entry to universities. Jews were excluded from the physics department, in particular, at the prestigious Moscow State University, because Soviet leaders did not trust them with nuclear rocket research. Unfortunately for Michael, astronomy fell under the rubric of physics.

Michael opted to study mathematics instead. But gaining acceptance to the math department at Moscow State, home of arguably the brightest mathematicians in the world, also proved exceedingly difficult. Discrimination there was administered by means of entrance exams for which Jews were tested in different rooms from other applicants—morbidly nicknamed "gas chambers"—and graded more harshly. Nevertheless, with help from a well-connected family friend, Michael was accepted and in 1970 graduated with an honors degree.

"I had all A's except for three classes where I got B's: history of the Communist Party, military training and statistics," he says. "But nobody would even consider me for graduate school because I was Jewish. That was normal." So Michael became an economist for GOSPLAN, the central planning agency. "I was trying to prove that, in a few years, living standards in Russia would be higher than in the United States," he says. "And I proved it. I know enough about math to prove whatever you want."

He continued to study mathematics on his own, sneaking into evening seminars at the university and writing research papers. After several were published, Brin began a doctoral thesis. At the time, a student in the Soviet Union could earn a doctorate without going to graduate school if he passed certain exams and an institution agreed to consider his thesis. Michael found two advisers, an official adviser, an ethnic Russian, and an informal Jewish mentor. ("Jews could not have Jewish advisers," he says.) With their help, he successfully defended his thesis at a university in Kharkov, Ukraine, but life didn't change much even after he received his Ph.D. He continued in his day job at GOSPLAN and received a 100-ruble raise. "I thought I was rich. Life was beautiful," he says with a wry chuckle.

For Genia, life in Moscow was also comfortable enough. She, too, had managed to overcome the entrance hurdles to attend Moscow State, graduating from the School of Mechanics and Mathematics. In a research lab of the Soviet Oil and Gas Institute, a prestigious industrial school, she worked alongside a number of other Jews. "I was content in my job and had many friends," she says. The Brins' encounters with institutional anti-Semitism did not extend to day-to-day interactions with colleagues and neighbors. Highly assimilated into Russian culture, they were part of the intelligentsia and had a circle of university-educated friends. Occupying a tiny, three-room apartment in central Moscow, 350 square feet in all, shared with Michael's mother, they were better off than many Muscovites who still lived in communal apartments. After Sergey was born, on August 21, 1973, the courtyard of their hulking five-story building became his playground. In keeping with Russian tradition, Sergey spent two hours in the morning and evening each day outdoors, regardless of the season.

As we talk at the bagel shop, Michael keeps careful watch on the time. Every so often he leaps from his chair and dashes outside. This isn't just for a smoke, although he does light up. He's also keeping close tabs on the parking meters, his and mine, and takes care when the time runs out to drop in more quarters.

. . .

THE HISTORY OF RUSSIAN JEWISH emigration in the mid-1970s can be neatly summarized in a joke from the era: Two Jews are talking in the street, a third walks by and says to them, "I don't know what you're talking about but yes, it's time to get out of here!"

"I've known for a long time that my father wasn't able to pursue the career he wanted," Sergey tells me. As a young boy, though, Sergey had only a vague awareness of why his family wanted to leave their native Russia. He picked up the ugly details of the anti-Semitism they faced bit by bit years later, he says. Nevertheless, he sensed, early on, all of the things that he wasn't: He wasn't Russian. He wasn't welcome in his own country. He wasn't going to get a fair shake in advancing through its schools. Further complicating his understanding of his Jewish identity was the fact that, under the ardently atheist Soviet regime, there were few religious or cultural models of what being Jewish was. The negatives were all he had.

Sergey is too young to remember the day, in the summer of 1977, when his father came home and announced that it was time for the family to emigrate. "We cannot stay here any more," he told his wife and mother. He had arrived at his decision while attending a mathematics conference in Warsaw. For the first time, he had been able to mingle freely with colleagues from the United

States, France, England and Germany. Discovering that his intellectual brethren in the West "were not monsters," he listened as they described the opportunities and comforts of life beyond the Iron Curtain. "He said he wouldn't stay, now that he had seen what life could be about," says Genia.

The couple knew, of course, the perils of applying for an exit visa. They could easily end up refuseniks, unable to find work, shunned, in perpetual limbo. Nobody had promised Michael a position abroad but he was confident he could find work in the West that was intellectually stimulating and would support the family. Genia, however, was unconvinced. They had lived in Moscow their entire lives. They had decent jobs and a young son. Was it worth it to try to leave? "I didn't want to go," she says. "It took a while for me and his mother to agree. I had a lot more attachments." It was up to Michael to do the convincing. "I was the only one in the family who decided it was really important to leave—not in some distant future," he says.

The Brins' story provides me with a clue to the origins of Sergey's entrepreneurial instincts. His parents, academics through and through, deny any role in forming their son's considerable business acumen—"He did not learn it from us, absolutely not our area," Michael says. Yet Sergey's willingness to take risks, his sense of whom to trust and ask for help, his vision to see something better and the conviction to go after it—these traits are evident in much of what Michael Brin did in circumventing the system and working twice as hard as others to earn his doctorate, then leave the Soviet Union.

For Genia, the decision ultimately came down to Sergey. While her husband admits he was thinking as much about his own future as his son's, for her, "it was 80/20 about Sergey." They formally applied for an exit visa in September 1978. Michael was promptly fired. Genia, who had obtained her job through a relative, had to quit to insulate him from any recrimination. "When he got a whiff of our intentions," she says, "he said 'please get out of there as soon as possible.' It had to be a secret from everybody at work, my real reason for leaving. So I lied to all of my coworkers that I was simply leaving my job because I got another job, where I would only have to be at work three days a week and the salary would be higher. I made up—totally made up—the name of a place where I was planning to work." There was no other job, of course, and suddenly they found themselves with no income. To get by, Michael translated technical books into English, but it was painstaking work. He also began to teach himself computer programming, having no expectation of getting an academic position if they ever got out. When Genia found temporary work, again lying about her situation, they shared responsibility for looking after Sergey, who stayed at home rather than attend a miserable Soviet pre-school.

And then they waited.

. . .

FOR MANY SOVIET JEWS, exit visas never came. But, in May 1979, the Brins were granted papers to leave the U.S.S.R. "We hoped it would happen," Genia says, "but we were completely surprised by how quickly it did." The timing was fortuitous: They were among the last Jews allowed to leave until the Gorbachev era.

Sergey, who turned six that summer, remembers what followed as simply "unsettling"—literally so. "We were in different places from day to day," he says. The journey was a blur. First Vienna, where the family was met by representatives of HIAS, the Hebrew Immigrant Aid Society, which helped thousands of Eastern European Jews establish new lives in the free world. Then, on to the suburbs of Paris, where Michael's "unofficial" Jewish Ph.D. advisor, Anatole Katok, had arranged a temporary research position for him at the Institut des Hautes Etudes Scientifiques. Katok, who had emigrated the year before with his family, looked after the Brins and paved the way for Michael to teach at Maryland.

When the family finally landed in America on October 25, they were met at New York's Kennedy Airport by friends from Moscow. Sergey's first memory of the United States was of sitting in the backseat of the car, amazed at all the giant automobiles on the highway as their hosts drove them home to Long Island.

The Brins found a house to rent in Maryland—a simple, cinder-block struc-ture in a lower-middle-class neighborhood not far from the university campus. With a $2,000 loan from the Jewish community, they bought a 1973 Ford Maverick. And, at Katok's suggestion, they enrolled Sergey in Paint Branch

Montessori School in Adelphi, Maryland.

Patty Barshay, the school's director, became a friend and mentor to Sergey and his parents. She invited them to a party at her house that first December ("a bunch of Jewish people with nothing to do on Christmas Day") and wound up teaching Genia how to drive. Everywhere they turned, there was so much to take in. "I remember them inviting me over for dinner one day," Barshay says, "and I asked Genia, 'What kind of meat is this?' She had no idea. They had never seen so much meat" as American supermarkets offer.

Another thing the Brins shared with thousands of other families emigrating to the West from the Soviet Union was the discovery that, suddenly, they were free to be Jews.

"Russian Jews lacked the vocabulary to even articulate what they were feeling," says Lenny Gusel, the founder of a San Francisco-based network of Russian-Jewish immigrants; many newcomers he encounters struggle with this fundamental change. "They were considered Jews back home. Here they were considered Russians. Many longed just to assimilate as Americans." Gusel's group, which he calls the "79ers," after the peak year of immigration in the 1970s, and its New York cousin, RJeneration, have attracted hundreds of 20- and 30-something immigrants who grapple with their Jewish identity. "Sergey is the absolute emblem of our group, the number one Russian-Jewish immigrant success story," he says.

The Brins were no different from their fellow immigrants in that being Jewish was an ethnic, not a religious experience. "We felt our Jewishness in different ways, not by keeping kosher or going to synagogue. It is genetic," explains Michael. "We were not very religious. My wife doesn't eat on Yom Kippur; I do." Genia interjects: "We always have a Passover dinner. We have a seder. I have the recipe for gefilte fish from my grandmother."

Religious or not, on arriving in the suburbs of Washington, the Brins were adopted by a synagogue, Mishkan Torah of Greenbelt, Maryland, which helped them acquire furnishings for their home. "We didn't need that much, but we saw how much the community helped other families," Genia says.

Sergey attended Hebrew school at Mishkan Torah for the better part of three years but hated the language instruction and everything else, too.

"He was teased there by other kids and he begged us not to send him any more," his mother remembers. "Eventually, it worked." The Conservative congregation turned out to be too religious for the Brins and they drifted. When a three-week trip to Israel awakened 11-year-old Sergey's interest in all things Jewish, the family inquired at another synagogue about restarting studies to prepare for a bar mitzvah. But the rabbi said it would take more than a year to catch up and Sergey, who didn't want to wait past his 13th birthday, abandoned the pursuit.

If there was one Jewish value the Brin family upheld without reservation, Michael says, it was scholarship. Sergey's brother—who in his younger years was more fond of basketball than homework—even got the notion that advanced degrees were mandatory for all professions. "Sam once asked us, 'Is it true that before you play in the N.B.A. you have to get a Ph.D.?'" recalls his dad. To which the professor couldn't resist replying, "Yes, Sam, that's it!"

Sergey attended Eleanor Roosevelt High School, a large public school in Greenbelt. He raced through in three years, amassing a year's worth of college credits that would enable him to finish college in three years as well. At the University of Maryland, he majored in mathematics and computer science and graduated near the top of his class. When he won a prestigious National Science Foundation scholarship for graduate school, he insisted on Stanford. (M.I.T. had rejected him.) Aside from the physical beauty of Stanford's campus, Sergey knew the school's reputation for supporting high-tech entrepreneurs. At the time, though, his focus was squarely on getting his doctorate.

What came next is Google legend. In the spring of 1995, during a prospective student weekend, Sergey met an opinionated computer science student from the University of Michigan named Larry Page. They talked and argued over the course of two days, each finding the other cocky and obnoxious. They also formed an instant connection, relishing the intellectual combat.

Like Sergey, Larry is the son of high-powered intellects steeped in computer science. His father, Carl Victor Page, a computer science professor at Michigan State University until his death in 1996, received one of the first Ph.D.s awarded in the field. His mother, Gloria, holds a master's

degree in computer science and has taught college programming classes. The two young graduate students also shared a Jewish background.
Larry's maternal grandfather made aliyah and lived in the desert town of
Arad near the Dead Sea, working as a tool and die maker, and his mother
was raised Jewish. Larry, however, brought up in the mold of his father,
whose religion was technology, does not readily identify as a Jew. He, too,
never had a bar mitzvah.

Larry and Sergey soon began working on ways to harness information on
the World Wide Web, spending so much time together that they took on a
joint identity, "LarryandSergey." By 1996, Larry had hit on the idea of using
the links between web pages to rank their relative importance. Borrowing
from academia the concept of citations in research papers as a measure of top-
icality and value, he and Brin applied that thinking to the Web: if one page
linked to another, it was in effect "citing" or casting a vote for that page. The
more votes a page had, the more valuable it was. The concept seems rather
obvious in retrospect, and today most search engines operate on this prin-
ciple. But, at the time, it was groundbreaking. Calling their new invention
Google—a misspelling of a very large number in mathematics—Larry and
Sergey shopped it around to various companies for the price of $1 million.

No one was interested. In the technology boom of the late 1990s, conventional thinking was that so-called web portals like Yahoo! and AOL,
which offered email, news, weather and more, would make the most
money. No one cared about search. But Sergey and Larry knew they were
on to something, so they decided to take leaves of absence from Stanford
and build a company themselves. Sergey's parents were skeptical. "We
were definitely upset," Genia says. "We thought everybody in his right
mind ought to get a Ph.D."

Soliciting funds from faculty members, family and friends, Sergey and
Larry scraped together enough to buy some servers and rent that famous
garage in Menlo Park. Their venture quickly bore fruit: After viewing a
quick demo, Sun Microsystems co-founder Andy Bechtolsheim (himself an
immigrant from Germany) wrote a $100,000 check to "Google, Inc." The
only problem was, "Google, Inc." did not yet exist—the company hadn't
yet been incorporated. For two weeks, as they handled the paperwork, the
young men had nowhere to deposit the money.

. . .

It is difficult to pinpoint the moment when Google became a true American phenomenon. Traditional measures, such as gracing the cover of *Time* magazine or being profiled on *60 Minutes*, seem irrelevant when it comes to the fast-moving world of the Internet. But there's no doubt about the date that Wall Street began to take the quirky California company seriously. It was April 29, 2004, when Google formally filed paperwork for its initial public offering of stock.

Two things shocked the investment world that day. First were the company's staggeringly large revenue and profit figures, which until then had been closely guarded secrets. No one had dreamed that the subtle text advertisements Google placed alongside search results—which many web users don't even recognize as ads—could be so profitable. Second was the ruthlessly earnest "founders' letter" that Sergey and Larry had included with the filing, which began by stating that Google was "not a conventional company" and did not intend to become one. They followed up that show of bravado by granting an interview to *Playboy* for publication during a mandatory "quiet period" before the public offering, when securities regulations restrict company executives' public comments. The misdeed prompted many to wonder whether the Google founders were careless and immature or just incorrigible troublemakers. It didn't help that they had decided to make it tough for Wall Street insiders to dominate the stock offering by selling shares via public auction—their way of making the process more democratic and transparent.

On August 16, 2004, its first day of trading, Google stock shot from $85 to $100 per share. In November of 2006 it crossed the $500 mark, a number seldom seen in stock market history and far above the share prices of rivals Microsoft and Yahoo! At that price, Sergey and Larry, who together hold a controlling interest in the company, each boast an estimated net worth of $15 billion.

What does that sort of money do to a 33-year-old? If you're Sergey, you buy a new house on the peninsula south of San Francisco, trade in your hybrid Toyota Prius for a fancier ride, and continue shopping at Costco. "From my parents, I certainly learned to be frugal and to be happy without very many things," Sergey tells me. "It's interesting—I still find myself not wanting to leave anything on the plate uneaten. I still look at prices. I try to force myself to do this less, not to be so frugal. But I was raised being happy with not so much." His parents say Sergey taught them to shop at Costco, too. "He bought us a membership," Michael says. "It's a store that he knows and understands."

Sergey also understands something about cooking, a skill he picked up on his own. "A month before leaving [for Stanford], he realized he didn't know how to cook, so he learned," his mother tells me. Now, he owns a pasta machine and often joins his father in the kitchen when he comes home to visit. His specialty is Chernobyl Chili—"45 minutes in the microwave."

The trappings of extreme wealth haven't passed Sergey by entirely. In 2005, he and Larry jointly purchased a Boeing 767 jet and had it refitted for personal use. Interior sketches of the "party airplane"—which has two staterooms, sitting and dining areas, a large galley and seating for 50—surfaced in *The Wall Street Journal* last July. At one point, according to the plane's designer, the Google founders got into a spat over Sergey's insistence on a "California" king-sized bed in his private cabin. CEO Schmidt had to mediate, telling them, "Sergey, you can have whatever bed you want in your room; Larry, you can have whatever bed you want in your bedroom. Let's move on."

While everyone I've talked to who knows them well repeats the same line— "They're good guys"—gossip web sites occasionally print rumors of Larry and Sergey's soirees in posh private clubs and other typical jet-setter antics. They are without a doubt two of the most eligible bachelors on Google Earth, but both are reported to be in serious relationships: Larry with Stanford graduate student Lucy Southworth, and Sergey with Anne Wojcicki, a healthcare investor and the sister of Google executive Susan Wojcicki, who owned the garage where Google got started. In a 2001 interview for the now-defunct web site Women. com, Genia said she hoped Sergey would find "somebody exciting who could be really interesting to him…[who] had a sense of humor that could match his." As one might expect, she also prefers that Sergey marry a Jewish girl. "I hope that he would keep it in mind," she confided.

. . .

THE TEN COMMANDMENTS IT'S NOT, but Google does operate with a moral code of sorts: "Don't Be Evil." The maxim is supposed to guide behavior at all levels of the company. When pressed for clarification, Eric Schmidt has famously said, "Evil is whatever Sergey says is evil."

One malevolent practice, in Google's view, is tampering with or otherwise censoring the list of results produced by a Google search. An early test of the Google founders' commitment to providing unfiltered information struck very close to home. The anti-Semitic web site "Jew Watch" appeared prominently in Google results for searches on the term "Jew," prompting some Jewish groups to demand that Google remove the defamatory site from the top of its listings. Google refused. Sergey said at the time, "I certainly am very offended by the site, but the objectivity of our rankings is one of our very important principles." As a compromise, Google displays a warning at the top of questionable pages entitled "Offensive Search Results," which links to a fuller explanation of Google's policy: "Our search results are generated completely objectively and are independent of the beliefs and preferences of those who work at Google."

The most telling measure of Google's moral code has come in China, the world's second largest Internet market, where an army of Communist Party bureaucrats actively monitors and censors the Internet. During months of intense debate at the Googleplex, Sergey, Larry and other executives weighed the vast profit potential of launching a China-based service against their opposition to the country's odious human rights abuses. Ever the computer geeks, Schmidt said they actually worked up an "evil scale." To their minds, operating a censored Google site in China was a lesser evil than providing spotty, substandard service from outside the country. The outcome also happened to favor the profit motive. Viewed against the backdrop of Sergey's distaste for authority, the decision to cave in to China's totalitarian leadership seems out of character.

Sergey's public comments on the matter have evolved to reflect this contradiction. While firmly defending the decision at first, he later acknowledged that Google had "compromised" its principles. "Perhaps now the principled approach makes more sense," he allowed in June, but added, "It's not where we chose to go right now."

How Google deals with such thorny matters as accommodating government requests for information is not merely of passing interest. As the world's dominant search engine, used some 300 million times daily, it marshals an immense amount of data about our collective interests, needs and desires. And that's not all. Because every search typed into Google is stored indefinitely and can often be traced to individual computer users, privacy advocates point out that clever government prosecutors or divorce lawyers could get their hands on our personal digital dossiers. Google's motto may be "Don't Be Evil," but it all depends into whose hands this information falls.

· · ·

DOES ANY COMPANY FOUNDED by two Jews, no matter how assimilated, necessarily retain some defining Jewish characteristics? The Google masterminds' penchant for pushing boundaries—without asking permission—might as well be called chutzpah. However you label it, it's an attitude that runs deeply through Google and may help explain why the company is embroiled in lawsuits over many of its new projects: the aggressive scanning of library books it doesn't own; display of copyrighted material; and copyright issues connected to its acquisition of YouTube, the online video site whose popularity rests in part on the availability of pirated television and movie clips.

Google's first employee and a number of other early hires were Jewish and, when the initial winter holiday season rolled around, a menorah rather than a Christmas tree graced the lobby. (The next year, there was a tree wrapped in Hanukkah lights.) Google's former chef, Charlie Ayers, cooked up latkes, brisket, tzimmes and matzoh ball soup for Hanukkah meals and turned the Passover seder into a Google tradition. To some, Google's emphasis on academic achievement—hiring only the best and the brightest and employing hundreds of Ph.D.s—could be considered Jewish. So, perhaps, could "Don't Be Evil." With its hint of tikkun olam, the Kabbalistic concept of "repairing the world" is evident in the company's commitment to aggressive philanthropy. Sergey and Larry have pledged $1 billion of Google's profits to the company's philanthropic arm, known as Google.org, which will funnel money both to nonprofit charities and companies that deal with global poverty, environmental issues and renewable energy.

Personal philanthropy is one area where Sergey intends to proceed cautiously. "I take the philosophical view that, aside from some modest stuff now, I am waiting to do the bulk of my philanthropy later, maybe in a few years, when I feel I'm more educated," he says. "I don't think it's something I have had time to become an expert at." Nevertheless, he and his parents do support a few charities. "There are people who helped me and my family out. I do feel responsible to those organizations," he says. One of them is HIAS, the immigrant aid group that helped the Brins come to the United States. Genia serves on its board and heads its project to create a digital record of Jewish immigrant archives.

Sergey's own Jewish sensibility is grounded in his family's experience. "I do somewhat feel like a minority," he says. "Being Jewish, especially in Russia, is one aspect of that. Then, being an immigrant in the U.S. And then, since I was significantly ahead in math in school, being the youngest one in a class. I never felt like a part of the majority. So I think that is part of the Jewish heritage in a way." Today, of course, being a young billionaire, he's again in a class by himself. "I don't feel comfortable being one of the crowd," he reflects. "It's kind of interesting—I really liked the schools that I went to, but I never rooted for the sports teams. I was never one of the crowd, supporting something or not. I like to maintain my independence."

I'm curious as to whether Sergey has been a target of anti-Semitism since he left the Soviet Union. "I've experienced it," he tells me. "Usually it is fairly subtle. People harp on all media companies being run by Jewish executives, with the implication of a conspiracy." As an example, he cites the entry about him in Wikipedia, the popular online encyclopedia that famously accepts submissions and edits from anyone. "The Wikipedia page about me will be subtly edited in an anti-Semitic way," he says.

He doesn't elaborate, so I later take a look myself. Wikipedia retains the old versions of each of its pages and in that archive I find a number of occasions where people have added, moved or deleted references to Sergey's Jewishness. Most seem harmless or ambiguous, but one jumps out. Several months ago, someone anonymously deleted a long-standing reference to the reason his parents had left Russia: "anti-Semitism."

"I think I'm fortunate that it doesn't really affect me personally," Sergey says of anti-Semitism. "But there are hints of it all around. That's why I think it is worth noting."

SEVERAL YEARS AGO, Sergey and Larry visited a high school for gifted math students near Tel Aviv. When they came onto the stage of the darkened auditorium, the audience roared, as if they were rock stars. Every student there, many of them immigrants like Sergey from the former Soviet Union, knew of Google.

Larry took the podium first, urging the students to maintain a "healthy disregard for the impossible," a favorite Google phrase. When it was Sergey's turn to speak, he began, to the crowd's delight, with a few words in Russian, which he still speaks at home with his parents.

"I have standard Russian-Jewish parents," he then continued in English. "My dad is a math professor. They have a certain attitude about studies. And I think I can relate that here, because I was told that your school recently got seven out of the top 10 places in a math competition throughout all Israel."

The students applauded their achievement and the recognition from Sergey, unaware that he was setting up a joke. "What I have to say," he continued, "is in the words of my father: 'What about the other three?'"

The students laughed. They knew where he was coming from. That Sergey has parlayed his talents and skills into unimaginable business success doesn't mean those "standard Russian-Jewish parents" are ready to let him off the academic hook. Genia still believes that "everybody in their right mind" ought to have a doctorate, and she and Michael are not joking when they tell me that they would like to see Sergey return to Stanford and finish what he started. ౧

4

THE PLAYWRIGHT'S POLITICS

Ted Merwin & David Zax • *October/November 2007*

TONY KUSHNER HAS CURLY BLACK HAIR, a high-pitched voice and an endearing gap between his teeth. He has barely begun to talk, but he already has a serious, intense look in his eyes, framed by large, round glasses.

His Manhattan office is not much larger than a walk-in closet, but the location, just off Union Square, seems appropriate. The playwright looks at home here, in a part of the city where rallies and political demonstrations have taken place since the middle of the 19th century and where radicals of every description have shouted themselves hoarse.

Kushner, 51, is a political playwright. Though he often writes about families (his 2004 musical *Caroline, or Change*, takes place largely in a Louisiana Jewish household), he is not predominantly an observer of familial relations. Though he sometimes writes about the supernatural (angels and spirits appear in his play, *Angels in America*), he will not be remembered as a teller of ghost stories. And though his recent foray into screenwriting involved several heart-pounding sequences with bombs and guns (he co-wrote the screenplay for 2005's *Munich*, about the Israeli revenge mission against the terrorists of the 1972 Munich Olympics), he is not principally a writer of suspense.

Rather, Kushner's writing concerns the downtrodden and oppressed. Themes recurring in his work are the struggles of gays, of Jews, of blacks——of gay Jews and gay blacks, sometimes——and other minorities for the justice he believes they are so often denied.

The young playwright was already making a name for himself as a writer and director in regional theater when he assailed the overweening optimism of the Reaganite 1980s with the sprawling, two-part *Angels in America: A*

Gay Fantasia on National Themes. "An epic for our epoch," according to *The Boston Globe*, *Angels* had its Broadway debut in 1993 when he was just 37. Kushner set it at a time when HIV/AIDS was spreading rapidly, yet few government officials were willing to acknowledge the disease existed. Interweaving stories of gay men sick with the disease, supernatural creatures and public figures like Roy Cohn and Ethel Rosenberg, the play asked searching questions about whether a new day had actually dawned in America, as the Reagan administration claimed. The play, which won the Pulitzer Prize for drama in 1993, became an anthem for gay liberation. In 1995, Kushner told *Mother Jones* that he "would hate to write anything that wasn't" part of a political movement. "I would like my plays to be of use to progressive people. I think preaching to the converted is exactly what art ought to do."

Kushner's contribution to political discourse is not limited to his plays; he is a regular at rallies and demonstrations and gives politically themed speeches at regional theaters, college graduations, and even his father's 80th birthday party. "Any culture is engaged in an incredibly complicated series of conversations at any moment," says Kushner, who has embraced the role of a public intellectual. Public intellectuals, he says, are "people who are willing to make their own personal journeys through those conversations available on a public level and to participate directly in these conversations." Kushner has been more than willing to do both.

Politically involved playwrights often meet skepticism. "I'm a dilettante, so, in a certain sense, why should anyone listen to me?" Kushner admits. But, of course, he has an answer ready. "Very recently, in the war in Iraq, we've been led straight into hell by a lot of experts who were very generous with their contempt for anyone who wasn't a policy expert...And there were a lot of non-experts who were saying exactly what was going to happen if we did this incredibly stupid and terrible thing."

Kushner doesn't want people to listen to him or admire his plays simply because of who he is or the prizes he's won. He considers this a Jewish characteristic, in a sense. In the rabbinic tradition, "you don't get attention just because somebody's elected you cardinal and you put on a big hat." Rather, for rabbinic Judaism, "knowledge is the seedbed and the foundation of power. If one isn't able to ask provocative, mind-expanding questions, then one has no business asking for anyone's attention."

Kushner has a demonstrated record of asking questions that might be worth our time. Some years ago he grew concerned with a certain central Asian country few Americans paid attention to. Reading newspaper accounts of an oppressive fundamentalist regime ruling that country, he thought to himself that any place in such dire circumstances was primed to explode. He set his next play, *Homebody/Kabul*, in that country, Afghanistan. It made mention of Osama bin Laden, and one character even spoke about the Taliban's coming to New York. *Homebody/Kabul* was about to enter rehearsals when the Twin Towers were hit in 2001.

Not long ago Kushner was rummaging through an old box when he came across a pink triangle badge, which reminded him of an argument with his father many years before.

When Kushner was growing up in Lake Charles, Louisiana, his family belonged to a Reform temple (so Reform, Kushner likes to quip, that it was virtually "reformed out of existence"). Anti-Semitism simmered just beneath the surface of the polite Southern society that surrounded them; when his father was appointed conductor of the local symphony, he had to overcome opposition from conservative Christians. Teachers at Tony's Episcopal school would drop the occasional anti-Semitic remark.

Kushner's personal trial, however, wasn't his Jewishness but his sexuality. The gangly boy with large glasses and an enormous Jewfro had found boys cuter than girls since the age of six. As many closeted gays do, he hid his feelings and even had a girlfriend. His freshman year at Columbia, in 1974, Kushner showed up at the university health center, hoping a therapist could help make him straight. It took three years for Kushner to come out of the closet, and he waited until he was 25 to tell his parents. His mother "cried for six months," he has said, and his father took it even harder.

By the mid-1980s, Kushner's father had at last begun to come around, if grudgingly, to accepting his son's homosexuality. But when he came to New York to visit and Tony insisted on wearing the pink triangle out to dinner to show his support for gay rights, his father protested. It's fine if you want to have sex with men, Kushner remembers his father saying, but why do you have to parade it in public?

Without knowing it, Kushner's father had actually been preparing his son for an argument like this for a long time. "Being Jewish was invaluable preparation for being gay," Kushner has said. When he decided to come out, "a little light bulb went off. I realized that I already knew how to do this; I'd been doing this all my life." His parents had taught their children that "you didn't have to take shit from people," as he once put it, and that they ought to insist on their dignity as Jews. His childhood as a member of one minority had prepared him for adulthood in another minority, to the point where he says, "I even knew how to argue with my parents about it."

That faded pink triangle—an emblem first used by the Nazis to label homosexuals in their concentration camps—reminds Kushner of the close connection between Jews' and gays' struggle for civil rights. "It was right there," he says, the unity of those struggles embodied in that badge. So once he came out, Kushner knew he could never again keep his sexuality a secret, and ironically, he has his father to thank for that belief. "I told him, you die if you stay in the closet. You die if you deny who you are. He had taught me that."

While being Jewish may have been good preparation for being gay, Kushner has found that being gay has at times made it hard to be Jewish. "When you're addressing yourself to Jewish religious tradition or any religious tradition, you address yourself to a tremendous amount of prejudice," he says. Judaism's sexual ethics, Kushner says, are "completely heterosexual and, in fact, homophobic in its oldest form." As a result, he and other gays are forced to reject certain elements of Judaism.

But where does that stop? "Can you really have a religion if it's simply a matter of writing your own law?" he asks. "Where is the law? And what does the law mean, and what do you agree to, what do you agree to give up? What do you feel it might be salutary to your soul to give up?"

At times, Kushner is unable to see any kind of resolution except to reject the parts of Judaism that seem like "repression cloaked in a religious disguise" and to embrace those that appeal to him. Still, he has found a Manhattan shul that is open and welcoming, and when he married editor Mark Harris in 2003, their wedding was decidedly Jewish. "I wanted a rabbi," he explains, "partly for sentimental reasons. I wanted to be married under a chuppah, I wanted to say the blessings, I wanted there to be Hebrew." The Kushner-Harris union was the first gay wedding to be featured in the "Vows" column of *The New York Times*; the accompanying photo shows the couple at Gabriel's, a Columbus Circle restaurant where they go for Italian food. "I wanted to have as Jewish a wedding as two men can have in an Italian restaurant."

. . .

KUSHNER IS FAR FROM universally loved. Conservative gay writer Andrew Sullivan, who also married recently, says that he "felt Kushner's AIDS plays tried to coerce human suffering into a cartoonish ideological rubric." Feminist critic Camille Paglia has called him a writer of "self-canonizing propaganda."

Certainly, Kushner made few Jewish friends last year with his work on the Steven Spielberg film *Munich*. In a 2006 op-ed in *The Los Angeles Times*, Kushner reported that a cousin, upon reading reviews of the film, asked him why he harbored "a secret plan to destroy Israel."

Munich questions the Mossad's extra-legal tactics in hunting down and killing Arabs thought to be linked to the massacre of Israeli athletes at the 1972 Olympics. Leon Wieseltier, *The New Republic*'s literary editor, called it "soaked in the sweat of its own even-handedness" and "desperate in not wanting to be charged with a point of view." Columnist Charles Krauthammer came down much harder: "Munich, the massacre, had only modest success in launching the Palestinian cause with the blood of 11 Jews. *Munich*, the movie, has now made that success complete 33 years later."

Such criticism is nothing new to Kushner. Ever since 2002, when he wrote in the liner notes to a Klezmatics album, *Possessed*, that "the founding of the State of Israel was for the Jewish people a historical, moral, political calamity," Kushner has been assailed for purported pro-Palestinian sympathies. When Brandeis University offered him an honorary degree in 2006, Morton Klein of the Zionist Organization of America tried to block the award, claiming that Justice Louis Brandeis would be "turning over in his grave" if he knew that a "hater" of Israel were being granted an honorary doctorate. Alvin H. Rosenfeld's recent, much-discussed essay for the American Jewish Committee, "'Progressive' Jewish Thought and the New Anti-Semitism," targets Kushner as one of a new breed of anti-Zionist Jewish intellectuals who are, in the words of British lawyer Anthony Julius, "proud to be ashamed to be Jews."

When he is asked about being called anti-Israel, Kushner's face is pained.

"These groups work very hard, by taking things out of context, to make you sound nuts," he says. He insists he is not anti-Israel: "Every time I've been to Jerusalem, I've been so excited that I can't breathe."

Kushner says he absolutely believes in Israel's right to exist, but he is wary of uncritical support and believes the involvement of American Jews in Israeli politics has been "mostly catastrophic." He thinks his role ought to be "to try to change the conversation here and make it possible for the U.S. government to adopt a sane policy that guarantees Israel's security but puts the Israelis and Palestinians on the road to creating a two-state solution and peaceful coexistence." He also doubts that Palestinian terrorism is caused by sheer evil, and hoped to illustrate this with *Munich*. The film, he says, "suggests, in a very Jewish way, that you can deplore someone's behavior without denying that the person is human and is motivated by recognizable and possibly even empathizable motives."

Kushner also believes—indeed knows—that anti-Semitism is real: "Anti-Semitism exists everywhere in the world—it has this weird endurance, and we have to be smart about it." But he doesn't feel that the state of Israel is the solution to ensuring the protection of the world's Jewry. "The solution to the problems of minorities in the world is not nationalism but equal protection under the law—which is not as comfortable-feeling as saying, 'We've got our own country now.' But, of course, we're learning over and over again that having your own country isn't necessarily so comfortable, either. Jews have done better in the diaspora than even in Israel, because pluralist democracy works."

The Jerusalem on the map (which Kushner thinks ought to be "a U.N. protectorate shared by the 957 religions that claim their origin within the city limits") is not where his heart turns for comfort. "My Jerusalem is the Equal Protection Clause of the 14th Amendment," he says.

· · ·

THE PAST SEVERAL YEARS have kept Kushner very busy. His recent work includes a new translation of Bertolt Brecht's *Mother Courage and Her Children*; *Wrestling With Zion*, an anthology of progressive Jewish writing about the Israeli-Palestinian conflict that he co-edited; and an adaptation of *Brundibar* (with Maurice Sendak), a children's opera written by a Czech Jew that was first performed in the Theresienstadt concentration camp.

Today, Kushner is at work on another project for Steven Spielberg—a screenplay about Abraham Lincoln—and he nearly has a first draft finished. "I just shoved everything else out of the way, because Lincoln is a very difficult subject to tackle....It's a gigantic subject, kind of an overwhelming subject," he says. In a way, though, it's a natural subject for Kushner, who considers the 16th president "the greatest democratic leader in the history of the world," a man with a deep "connection to tragedy," and "one of the greatest writers this country has ever produced."

He especially admires Lincoln's Second Inaugural Address, which suggests that God may will the Civil War to continue—despite its horrors—"until all the wealth piled by the bondsman's two hundred and fifty years of unrequited toil shall be sunk, and until every drop of blood drawn with the lash shall be paid by another drawn with the sword."

"To say that to this country that had suffered so much, at the moment of your greatest political triumph, is astounding," says Kushner, his voice rising with admiration, reminding a listener that Lincoln himself also was said to have had a high-pitched but penetrating voice. "You can't imagine any modern political leader being that honest," Kushner concludes. There is no current politician he admires so much as Lincoln, he says.

Kushner has enjoyed his recent foray into Hollywood; in addition to working with Spielberg, he collaborated with Mike Nichols on a TV mini-series version of *Angels,* which won a record 11 Emmys in 2003. But he insists that once he is finished with the screenplays he's at work on now, he wants to return to the theater. Screenwriting, he has said, is more of a narrative art, whereas playwriting (the form with which he is most comfortable) trades in dialogue and dialectic, and is more Talmudic in its focus on inquiry and argument. He also finds film audiences dizzyingly huge (more people saw *Angels* in one night on HBO than in its entire Broadway run). "The nice thing about theater is that you can really, with a fair degree of accuracy, tell yourself that the people you're writing for are familiar, and sort of haimish. That you're writing for the mishpocha," he says.

· · ·

IN 1992, CRITIC FRANK RICH wrote in *The New York Times*: "Some visionary playwrights want to change the world. Some want to revolutionize the theater. Tony Kushner, the remarkably gifted 36-year-old author of *Angels in America*, is that rarity of rarities: a writer who has the promise to do both."

Kushner's good friend, the director Oskar Eustis, often likes to discuss the intimate relationship between theater and politics. In the 2006 documentary on Kushner, *Wrestling With Angels*, Eustis points out that democracy and drama arose almost simultaneously in ancient Greece, since "the same emotion that is required for theater to work is the emotion that is required for democracy to work: the idea we need to care about each other's experience." Kushner has a remarkable ability "to care about and understand people who are dramatically different from himself," says Eustis, an ability which gives him "a size of vision" unmatched in other living playwrights.

Since Kushner is so good at getting in the minds of others, it seems worth tossing him an old interview standby: If he could be anyone at any moment in history, who would he be?

He takes the question far more seriously than one might have imagined. Perhaps he would have been George W. Bush on the eve of invading Baghdad, and stopped the war from happening. Perhaps he would have been the assassin who nearly blew up Hitler, but hadn't placed the bomb near enough.

Or perhaps, to share in the thrill of it, he would have been at the 1963 March on Washington. But then he abruptly reconsiders, deciding he has "never wanted to be at any other time than the time I'm in, as terrible as this time is." He quotes Bertolt Brecht: "Don't start from the good old things, but the bad new ones." Turning the clock back, Kushner adds, "is the essence of reactionary politics—it always produces horror."

But his mind makes a final characteristic leap from politics to art: "I would love to be Shakespeare writing *Hamlet*. It would be nice to know what that felt like. That would be cool." ⌀

5

JONATHAN STUART LEIBOWITZ (AKA) JON STEWART

Jeremy Gillick & Nonna Gorilovskaya • *November/December 2008*

ON JANUARY 11, 1999, a nervous 37-year-old comedian who could have passed for a college student settled into a host's chair that was too high, wearing a gray suit that looked too large. "Honestly, I feel like this is my bar mitzvah," he told actor Michael J. Fox, the guest sitting opposite him. "I've never worn something like this, and I have a rash like you wouldn't believe."

The rookie was Jon Stewart, and he was making his debut as the anchorman of Comedy Central's two-year-old *The Daily Show*. It was not his dream job: That one had gone to his predecessor Craig Kilborn, who had taken his frat-boy act to CBS' *Late Late Show*—one of several gigs for which Stewart had been passed over.

Stewart then proceeded to dole out *The Daily Show*'s usual sophomoric fare: That night, it was the engagement announcement of cartoon characters Popeye and Olive Oyl (complete with mandatory wedding night joke). The show's celebrity correspondent filed an interview with the aging actors who played munchkins in *The Wizard of Oz*—"dwarf porn" and "dwarf tossing" were among the topics. But even on day one, the best part of the show was Stewart's commentary on the headlines, then consumed by President Bill Clinton's impeachment trial. "The important issue facing the U.S. Senate is how can it take a pointless, tawdry trial whose outcome has already been decided and make it last for six hilarious, humiliating months," he intoned.

During the following year, the show morphed into something altogether more edgy, showcasing Stewart's knack for thoughtful political satire. Although the program hasn't cast off all silliness and vulgarity, *The Daily Show with Jon Stewart* now wields a political influence far beyond its audience of nearly two million. Monday through Thursday, on a glitzy news set in New York City, the now graying anchorman—aided by a stable of faux correspondents wearing expressions of gravitas—spoofs politicians and America's 24-hour media culture. The method behind the madness? What Stewart, also the executive producer, and his writers call "fake news:" a humorous take on real events in a format that resembles "straight" news programs.

The Daily Show's audience is one of television's youngest—only 23 percent of viewers are 50 or older—and one of the best informed—even more so than viewers of CNN, C-SPAN and Fox, according to a 2008 Pew Research Center study. As a result, politicians, A-list actors, public intellectuals and pretty much anyone pitching a book, regardless of ideological persuasion, compete for spots on the nightly interview segment. The well-read Stewart has talked globalization and religion with former British Prime Minister Tony Blair and, over tea and Twinkies, questioned then-Pakistani President Pervez Musharraf about Osama bin Laden's whereabouts. Vice President Dick Cheney's wife, Lynne, regally swept in when her memoir came out, presenting Stewart with a Darth Vader statue and explaining that it was "an old family heirloom." (Dick Cheney is known as "Darth Cheney" on the show.) Actress Angelina Jolie has appeared, as have Senators Barack Obama and John McCain. Senator Hillary Clinton (whom *The Daily Show* has called "the first viable presidential candidate with a working uterus") scheduled one of her visits via satellite from Texas on the eve of the crucial 2008 Texas and Ohio primaries.

The Daily Show with Jon Stewart enjoys effusive critical and popular acclaim and has won 11 Emmy Awards. At forty-five, the once obscure Comedy Central comedian has become a media heavyweight. Last year, a Pew survey found Stewart to be one of the most admired journalists in America, tied at number four with news legends Dan Rather and Tom Brokaw. This year, *Forbes* listed him as one of the world's most powerful celebrities, with an annual income pegged at $14 million, and *The New York Times* asked: "Is Jon Stewart the most trusted man in America?"

As his star has risen, Stewart, born Jonathan Stuart Leibowitz, has also become an ambassador of Jewishness. Dispensing Jewish humor like a tic, Stewart's impish grin, self-deprecating punch lines and jokey cultural references are a staple of the show. He has referred to himself as "Jewey Von

Jewstein" and cracked wise on Jewish noses, circumcision, anti-Semites, Jews who play baseball (a short list), Israel as "Heebie Land" and his grandma at Passover. When it comes to Jewish and Israeli politics, he stomps where WASPier comedians fear to tread. But although he regularly brings up the fact that he is Jewish, he rarely speaks earnestly about his Jewish upbringing or what being Jewish means to him.

. . .

IN 1960, DON AND MARIAN LEIBOWITZ moved to New Jersey from New York City so that Don, a physicist, could be closer to his workplace at RCA Labs in Princeton. They settled in Lawrenceville, just down Route 206 from Princeton. The couple had two boys—Larry (who attended Princeton University and now, as group executive vice president of the New York Stock Exchange's Euronext, is a big player on Wall Street) and Jon, two years Larry's junior, born in a New York City hospital on November 28, 1962.

The Leibowitzes were a typical well-educated middle class Jewish family of the time. Marian, a teacher turned creative educational consultant, was the daughter of Nathan Laskin, a struggling immigrant who owned a series of small businesses in New York. Laskin came to the United States from Tianjin, China, where his family was in the fur business. Don's father was a cab driver in New York City, and his grandfather owned a shoe store on Irvington Street on the Lower East Side. "My father's father was very religious, Orthodox, perhaps to an extreme," recalls Don Leibowitz, now an adjunct professor of physics and liberal learning at The College of New Jersey, where he is the faculty advisor to the Secular Student Alliance. "When we visited his store, he would pinch my cheek and make me recite prayers."

Lawrenceville wasn't exactly a hotbed of Jewish life. Jon attended a yeshiva kindergarten in nearby Trenton, then joined his brother at the local public school. Stewart has recalled being punched in seventh grade and taunted as "Leibotits" and "Leiboshits." "I didn't grow up in Warsaw, but it's not like it wasn't duly noted by my peers that's who I was—there were some minor slurs," he said in a 2002 interview with *The New Yorker*'s Tad Friend.

Stewart's comedic streak and verbal agility was evident at an early age. "I was very little, so being funny helped me have big friends," Stewart explained in a 1994 *People* interview. "Jon is most like my father," Marian

Leibowitz told the *Trenton Times* in 2006. "[My father] was very funny and, when he was young, he made extra money entertaining in nightclubs in China." Stewart and Nathan Laskin were especially close.

While Larry's bar mitzvah was held at an upscale hotel in Somerville, Jon's was not. When he was 11, family circumstances had changed: Don Leibowitz moved out of the family home. "We had separated and the bar mitzvah, to keep the costs down, was at the Jewish Center," says Leibowitz, who is remarried and has two sons from his second marriage. He and Stewart are estranged.

At Lawrence High School, Stewart played on the varsity soccer team and gained a reputation as a funny guy. Not everyone on the staff appreciated his humor, but Selma Litowitz, his Jewish English teacher who died in 2005, got it. "He has said that she was the first who recognized that his humor was something that he could make a living at," says Debra Frank, the teacher's daughter. The Litowitzes lived on the same street—Glenn Avenue—as the Leibowitzes. In 2001, Stewart came back to his high school to emcee a benefit concert in Selma Litowitz's honor to raise funds for Parkinson's Disease research. "His opening joke," says Frank, "was that, for many years, he thought that Jews had to live alphabetically."

By high school, Stewart was already conversant in politics. He has recalled that he was "left-leaning" and "very into Eugene Debs," the perennial Socialist Party candidate for U.S. president in the early 20th century. For a mock debate, Stewart was assigned to play another presidential candidate whose politics were light years away from those of Debs': Ronald Reagan. "I had to defend increased military spending," Stewart told *George* magazine in 2000.

Stewart graduated in 1980, reportedly third in his class, and was voted "best sense of humor." "He was very funny, not funny in the sense that he would tell funny stories, more quick, witty," says Larry Nichol, Stewart's 12th grade English teacher. "He'd always be saying something on the way out the door as the bell was ringing."

· · ·

"I CAME TO WILLIAM AND MARY because as a Jewish person, I wanted to explore the rich tapestry of Judaica that is Southern Virginia," Jon Stewart joked as he accepted an honorary doctorate at the College of William and

Mary's 2003 graduation ceremony, wearing a gray sweatshirt beneath his academic robe. "Imagine my surprise when I realized 'The Tribe' was not what I thought it meant."

"The Tribe" refers to the school's athletic teams, and that Tribe indeed drew Stewart to this historic southern school, not an altogether obvious choice for a Jewish kid from New Jersey. In the 1980s, North-South tensions could still be felt on this conservative campus, which boasted traditions such as the Yule Log Ceremony, where the president dons a Santa outfit and reads *How the Grinch Stole Christmas* to the student body.

As in high school, Stewart was acknowledged as a funny man, although no one imagined that his future held a career in comedy. "He was always the locker room cut-up, but we've had other locker room cut-ups who haven't gone on to be comedians," Albert says.

Between traveling for matches and a rigorous academic load, there wasn't much time for soccer players to get into trouble. Beers at local delis, MTV, video games and occasional concerts provided their primary entertainment. "Jon was very popular with girls and dated some very attractive women in college," recalls John Rasnic, Stewart's college roommate and soccer teammate.

Rasnic remembers at least one incident in which Stewart bumped up against anti-Semitism. During a game against Randolph-Macon College, a liberal arts school in Virginia, Stewart was called a kike. "Jon was a little upset, I think, perhaps a bit surprised, but he didn't let it bother him," Rasnic says.

In 1983, Albert recruited Stewart for the Pan American Maccabi Games in São Paulo, Brazil, a lead-up to the World Maccabiah Games, the Jewish version of the Olympics. Stewart started for the U.S. team and, as usual, entertained as well. "He created a little bit of levity," says David Coonin, one of Stewart's Maccabi teammates, "but everybody was always a little afraid of messing with Jon because he was so quick-witted."

The 10-day trip included a Shabbat dinner, parties, Brazilian and Israeli dancing and skeptical Latin American Jews. "When we walked out on the soccer field, they called us 'gringos,'" says Fred Schoenfeld, co-chair of the Pan American Games that year. "They wanted to know if we knew how to play." The U.S. team proved itself by winning four games, losing only to Brazil in the finals. "After that, they no longer called us 'gringos.'"

On the surface, Stewart seems to have been well integrated into college life, but as an adult, he would describe his William and Mary days as "miserable" and himself as "a lost person." Stewart pledged a fraternity but dropped out, reportedly over objections to the hazing. Having started as a chemistry major, he switched to psychology after two years. "Apparently there's a right and wrong answer in chemistry; whereas in psychology, you can say whatever you want as long as you write five pages," Stewart quipped to *60 Minutes* in 2001.

Another source of frustration was Reagan's election during Stewart's freshman year. "We always talked politics," says Mike Flood, who played soccer with Stewart. "Neither of us was a particularly strong Reagan fan."

Stewart scored ten goals for William and Mary, but his hopes for a pro soccer career were dashed by injuries. "Toward the end of his career, he blew out his knee," says his father. Still, Stewart's legacy on The Tribe soccer team lives on in the form of the Leibo award, given annually in recognition of good humor and hard work.

After graduating from William and Mary in 1984, Stewart returned to New Jersey and kicked around at a number of odd jobs. He worked as a bartender at Lawrenceville's Franklin Corner Tavern, sorted live mosquitoes for the New Jersey Department of Health and was a puppeteer for special needs schoolchildren. Then in 1986, he sold his car and moved to New York to try stand-up comedy.

"When he finally decided to become a comedian, it was a little bit of a shock," Marian Leibowitz said in her *Trenton Times* interview. "But he was going to New York. He wasn't going to China. I decided I wasn't going to be the person to discourage him."

In 1987, the young comedian known as Jon Leibowitz scored a gig at the Bitter End in the West Village—a comedy club where his idol, Woody Allen, had once performed. As he was being introduced, the emcee mangled the pronunciation of his name, prompting him to rename himself then and there, he told *The New Yorker*. But he also hinted at other reasons, such as "some leftover resentment at my family," presumably referring to his strained relationship with his father.

The pronunciation of his name was not the only thing to go awry that first night at the Bitter End. Stewart made it only half way through his act. "Legend has it that Jon bombed," says Wendy Wall, who had booked him at the club. "But I really wouldn't say he 'bombed.' It was one in the morning. It's not easy with a crowd like that. It was obvious to me that he was funny." Wall invited him back for a second night.

After becoming a regular at New York's Comedy Cellar, he broke into television with an uncredited TV writing gig on *Caroline's Comedy Hour* on the A&E network and in 1992 landed a spot as the host of MTV's *You Wrote It, You Watch It*. Along the way he picked up a powerful fan, David Letterman, and became a frequent guest on Letterman's *Late Night* on NBC, often sporting a tough-guy leather jacket. When Letterman decamped to CBS, Stewart was a contender to replace him as *Late Night* host but lost out to Conan O'Brien. Still, MTV liked him, and in 1993 tapped him to host his own talk show, *The Jon Stewart Show*, which quickly became the second-highest rated program on the network. The show lasted two seasons.

Stewart's career slowly rolled on. He starred in *Jon Stewart: Unleavened* for HBO in 1996 and went on to score what are generally considered to have been mediocre guest-star appearances on sitcoms including *Newsradio, Spin City* and *The Nanny*, as well as roles in big-screen comedies like Adam Sandler's *Big Daddy*. He was more successful playing "himself"—a young comic who is brought in to replace an older mentor—on the pseudo-realistic *The Larry Sanders Show*. In one episode, Stewart flouts the censors and airs a skit featuring a character dressed up as Hitler. The inspiration came from a rehearsal sketch for Stewart's earlier talk show, in which Hitler tries to soften his image. "I don't know what I was afraid of. These are delicious!" comedian Dave Attell's Hitler proclaims after biting into a bagel.

Stewart's studio audience had booed and the skit was shelved, but it later turned into a hilarious bit of back-story and the basis for an essay, "Adolf Hitler: The Larry King Interview," in Stewart's 1998 book, *Naked Pictures of Famous People*. In it, the former fuhrer accepts the blame for his past actions and psychoanalyzes why his plan for world domination failed. "What do I do? I deport or kill all my best scientists...The Jews were some of my best technical people. It's classic fear of success," "Hitler" reasons.

• • •

BY 1998, STEWART HAD done standup. He'd done movies. He'd done TV. He'd published a best-selling book. He'd had—and lost—a show. But he had never really found his niche until, at age 37, he replaced Kilborn on *The Daily Show* in 1999. After a slightly bumpy beginning, Stewart began to lead the show away from its celebrity focus. He came into his own with the show's arch and sardonic coverage of the presidential election grandiosely labeled "Indecision 2000."

The show quickly drew the eyeballs of political junkies and earned a Peabody award, one of broadcast media's highest honors. "It was in the year 2000 that Jon Stewart officially became a public intellectual," says Robert Thompson, who directs the Bleier Center for Television and Popular Culture at Syracuse University.

Then came September 11, 2001. When Stewart came back on the air nine days later, he opened with a somber, halting speech that addressed the sudden absurdity of his jester role as well as its importance. "They said to get back to work, and there were no jobs available for a man in the fetal position," he said. "We sit in the back and we throw spitballs—never forgetting the fact that it is a luxury in this country that allows us to do that." Stewart choked up, tears in his eyes, and turned to the significance of carrying on:

"The view from my apartment was the World Trade Center. Now it's gone. They attacked it. This symbol of American ingenuity and strength and labor and imagination and commerce and it is gone. But you know what the view is now? The Statue of Liberty. The view from the south of Manhattan is now the Statue of Liberty. You can't beat that."

It was a long way from the Bitter End. It was, actually, a beginning: the unwitting kickoff of Jon Stewart as trusted national figure. With the wars in Afghanistan and Iraq, the show became a place where viewers came not just to laugh but also to be informed. The guest list grew weightier, expanding to include the Iranian-American religious scholar Reza Aslan, the late David Halberstam and newsmen Bill Moyers and Ted Koppel. "When all the news guys were walking on eggshells, Jon was hammering those questions about WMDs," recalls Thompson. "That's the kind of thing CNN and CBS should have been doing."

The Daily Show continues to blend the fake anchor shtick with fake news skits, "reported" by zany correspondents such as Samantha Bee, Wyatt Cenac,

Jason Jones, Aasif Mandvi, Rob Riggle and John Oliver. Where once Stewart could be as clownish as his reporters, he now plays calm. He still curses and goofs around, but he never strays far from being the voice of authority.

. . .

IT'S IMPOSSIBLE TO WATCH *The Daily Show* without quickly divining that Stewart is Jewish. "Stewart brings a sharpness of wit and a clear desire to never let the audience forget who he is by bringing his Jewishness up again and again," observes Moshe Waldoks, a rabbi in Brookline, Massachusetts, and co-editor of *The Big Book of Jewish Humor*. His cultural Jewishness, that is: Stewart regularly hosts *The Daily Show* on Yom Kippur, the holiest day in the Jewish calendar. (A New York Mets fan, Stewart did name one of his pit bulls Shamsky, after Art Shamsky, a Mets player who declined to play on Yom Kippur.)

Well-versed in Jewish affairs, he is the first to admit that his knowledge of the religion doesn't run deep. "I'm not a religious scholar," Stewart conceded to viewers in 2001. "Let's face facts: Very few people would confuse me with Maimonides." He gently pokes fun at his own lack of observance. "I fasted today, not out of any religious duty but because I don't want to let a day go by where I can't feel worse about myself. So Happy Yom Kippur to you!" Stewart wished his audience in 2003.

Nevertheless, his satire reverberates with a Jewish sensibility. "We have a long tradition of important Jewish comedians, all dealing with social and political issues," says Arthur Asa Berger, a professor of communications at San Francisco State University and author of the book *Li'l Abner: A Study in American Satire*, about the comic strip by the famed humorist Al Capp (born Alfred Gerald Caplin). Stewart's lampooning of America's political and media elites also has Jewish roots. "I think that there is such a thing as a Jewish psyche, a sense of the prophetic tradition, of speaking truth to power," says Waldoks.

Stewart himself counts Woody Allen (born Allan Stewart Konigsberg) and Lenny Bruce (born Leonard Alfred Schneider) as well as George Carlin and Richard Pryor among his influences. It's worth noting that *Seinfeld*, the show Stewart holds up as the gold standard for his own, has often been called the world's most famous Jewish comedy in which the word Jew was rarely heard. While Stewart is far more open about his Jewishness than Jerry Seinfeld, his humor is not as centered around it as, for example, Sarah Silverman's, who styles herself as a Jewish American princess.

Nor is he angrily anti-religion like Bill Maher, the half-Jewish, half-Catholic agnostic who recently brought America the film *Religulous* and who mercilessly attacks religion on his HBO show, *Real Time with Bill Maher*. "I don't have a problem with religion," Stewart once explained to Larry King. "I think that religion provides a lot of people with comfort and solace, but you know, I think what people who aren't that religious object to is [the belief] that the only way to find values is through religion."

Religious fundamentalism often crops up as a target in Stewart's comedy. In 1999, soon after he began hosting *The Daily Show,* ultra-Orthodox protesters heckled a co-ed group of Reform rabbis for praying together at the Western Wall. "Ultra-Orthodox Jews, desperately fearful of biblical cooties, got all Jewier-than-thou when they discovered that a handful of Reform Jews who actually allow their women to do something other than breed and cook also had the chutzpah to be praying nearby," he said. "Ultra-Orthodox Jews believe themselves superior to other Jews, claiming the Word was handed to them directly, right before [God] handed us big noses and took away all our athletic ability."

Like clockwork, Stewart mentions Jewish holidays throughout the year— like the night he joked about the midnight apple drop into a bowl of honey at Times Square on Rosh Hashanah. Another time, on *Larry King Live*, he said: "Who amongst us hasn't thought around Hanukkah, 'Oh, you're celebrating the birth of your Savior, and we're celebrating the fact that the oil lasted longer than we thought it would—what value!'"

The show even gets Jews laughing at sacred cows of all sorts. Stewart is not anti-Israel: "I'm a Jewish guy," he said during a 1996 standup routine. "I've been to Israel; I'm really glad it's there." But certainly Israel gets its share of *Daily Show* attention. Take the preface to John Oliver's 2001 interview with Dan Gillerman, then Israel's ambassador to the United Nations. Oliver, the tongue-in-cheek British correspondent, pointed to the Holocaust, Spanish Inquisition and pogroms as evidence that "Jews seem to have trouble getting along with people, so it was better to get them their own place." Later, Oliver asked Gillerman to put to rest the "nasty conspiracy theory…that your country is run by Jews.'"

After presidential candidates Clinton, McCain and Obama spoke at the 2008 annual Washington conference hosted by AIPAC, Stewart mocked all three for pandering: McCain talked about having traveled to Israel with Joe Lieberman ("You don't need to bring your own Jew"); Clinton referenced a passage from Isaiah ("She knows a Jew from the Bible!"); and Obama recalled a Jewish-American camp counselor ("That's one step from 'Hey, I rented *Yentl* once!'"). After waiting to hear some "constructive criticism" of Israeli policies that "may not be in the best interest of the world," Stewart rolled clips of silence and went for the kill: "Oh! I forgot! You can't say anything remotely critical of Israel and still get elected president! Which is funny, because you know where you can criticize Israel? Israel!"

Although the topic doesn't come up often, it's also evident where Stewart stands on intermarriage. In 2000, he married Tracey McShane, a veterinary technician and a Catholic. Stewart, who does *The New York Times* crossword puzzle daily, popped the question with a puzzle of his own. The paper's "Puzzle Master," Will Shortz, found Stewart a puzzle creator for the occasion.

The Stewarts (they changed their names legally in 2001) live in a loft in lower Manhattan and have two children. Nathan Thomas Stewart, four, is named after his grandfather. Maggie Rose Stewart is two. As Stewart told Tony Blair on *The Daily Show* in a September 2008 interview, "My wife is Catholic. I'm Jewish. It's very interesting; we're raising the children to be sad."

• • •

PERHAPS MORE THAN ANY OTHER SATIRIST, Stewart commands the attention—and respect—of folks in the "real" media. *New Yorker* editor David Remnick and PBS' Bill Moyers consider him an important media critic. *The Daily Show's* trademark editing technique of playing back-to-back clips of politicians contradicting themselves has garnered that highest form of flattery: imitation by the very networks Stewart mocks.

Nevertheless, Stewart insists that he and his staff are just a bunch of "monkeys making jokes." In particular, he dismisses suggestions that *The Daily Show* aims to do anything more than make people laugh. On October 15, 2004, when he went on CNN's *Crossfire*—a then-popular target of *The Daily Show* because of its screaming matches between pundits—Stewart begged hosts Paul Begala, a former Clinton advisor, and Tucker Carlson, the young bow-tied conservative journalist, to "stop hurting America" with their "partisan hackery." Carlson would have none of it. He pushed back, attacking Stewart for a softball interview with Democratic presidential nominee John Kerry.

An incredulous Stewart responded by reminding Carlson that their shows were not in the same category. "You're on CNN," he said. "The show that leads into me is puppets making crank phone calls." The exchange was a YouTube sensation, and Stewart was tagged the winner; few disagreed with his statement that something is really wrong with the fourth estate if, as he put it, "news organizations look to Comedy Central for their cues on integrity."

"Stewart panders exclusively" to his liberal, young audience, insists Carlson, now at MSNBC: "He's a show for the Democratic Party. He sucks up to power rather than confront it." However, Stewart's interviewing style has been called into question by his admirers as well. Lately, there have been instances where Stewart has been a more aggressive interviewer, squaring off with McCain and Blair over the Iraq war. But it is unrealistic to expect comedians to carry out the job of newsmen, says Syracuse University's Thompson. "Jon Stewart is not a journalist. He doesn't claim to be, and when he says he's not we should believe it. His interviews are in the tradition of Johnny Carson. Basically he's polite, at times deferential. He behaves in the interviews like a well-brought-up young man."

Stewart denies that *The Daily Show* has a political agenda. His Comedy Central colleague Stephen Colbert—whose mock Bill O'Reilly persona on *The Daily Show* led to a spin-off created by Stewart's Busboys Productions called *The Colbert Report*—views Stewart as an equal-opportunity satirist. "Jon is admirably balanced," Colbert has said, explaining that Stewart always tries to get at "the true intention of the person speaking, left or right" in order "to be able to honestly mock."

Stewart makes no secret of his impatience with President Bush, known on the show by the superhero moniker "The Decider" or as "Still President Bush." Stewart recently told *The New York Times* that he is looking forward to the end of the Bush era "as a comedian, as a person, as a citizen, as a mammal." But perhaps out of respect for his comedian-cum-journalist role and unlike other comedians like Silverman, an activist for Democrats, and Jackie Mason, an outspoken Republican, he stays somewhat mum about his own political preferences, although it is clear that he leans Democrat. (The only documented recipient of his financial largesse is New York Congressman Anthony Weiner, a Democrat and Big Apple mayoral candidate, with whom Stewart roomed after college.)

The Pew study analyzed the show's content during the summer and fall of 2007, concluding that "Stewart's humor targeted Republicans more than three times as often as Democrats. The Bush administration alone was the focus of 22 percent of the segments." Although this percentage is likely to change when a Democratic administration comes to power, Democrats do not escape his tongue-lashing, even if it is to criticize them for not being Democratic enough. There is a sort of liberal angst in his characterizations of Democrats as "at best ewoks," a reference to cuddly, somewhat hapless *Star Wars* creatures.

In the run-up to the 2004 elections, Stewart indicated that he would vote for John Kerry. Although no one imagines that Stewart cast a vote for McCain, who supports the Iraq war, McCain was a guest on the show 13 times, far more than either Clinton or Obama. Many of McCain's guest spots were via satellite from his Straight Talk Express bus during low points in his primary campaign, providing him with much needed media exposure. "John McCain is someone for whom I have great respect," Stewart told Larry King last February.

Despite his effort to be a fair and balanced mocker, Stewart's reputation as the "most trusted man in America" should be taken with a grain of salt. Such stature is not unusual for a comedian, says Nicholas Lemann, the dean of the Graduate School of Journalism at Columbia University. "Johnny Carson in his heyday, you could make that statement about." Lemann warns against generalizing about how far that trust spreads beyond Stewart's core audience. "I think that's a kind of a blue-state perspective and youth perspective. To many of my cousins in Louisiana, Rush Limbaugh is the most trusted man in America."

Left or right, people acknowledge that Stewart is very funny. Part of his appeal may be his Jewishness and the fact that Jews are still perceived as outsiders, says Moshe Waldoks. At the same time, Stewart personifies a trend in which younger American Jews have become more open about being Jewish. "I think like the Jewishness of many people today, Stewart's Jewishness is not expressed in the synagogue or ritually but in this new place, which is the public square," adds Waldoks.

In the public square, Stewart may be the perfect Jewish ambassador for our times: smart but not arrogant, extremely funny but not mean—a valedictorian, most popular, best-looking and class clown all wrapped into one.

So, is Jon Stewart, to ask that annoying question, good for the Jews? As Fareed Zakaria, the editor of *Newsweek International*, puts it, "Are you serious? How could Jon Stewart not be good for the Jews?" ☙

6

THE CURIOUS CASE OF WALTER MOSLEY

Johanna Neuman • *September/October 2010*

HE SHOWS UP WITHOUT HIS TRADEMARK HAT. But then, Walter Ellis Mosley is all about defying expectations. The son of a black father and a Jewish mother, the 58-year-old Mosley is one of former President Bill Clinton's favorite writers. His output careens from mystery novels to science fiction, from left-wing political treatises to existential erotica.

His passions, like his characters, defy categorization. Ezekiel "Easy" Rawlins, a hard-bitten black private detective and a World War II veteran who encounters crime and racial animus in post-war South Central Los Angeles, and Leonid McGill, an ex-boxer and a private investigator on the tough side of New York in a new millennium, are profiles in contradiction.

I meet Mosley at Dish, a trendy bar in Washington, DC's Foggy Bottom. Perhaps sensing Mosley's celebrity, the bartender agrees to seat us even though the restaurant is not yet open for the evening. We perch on high stools in the receding light of the late afternoon, drinking espresso from white porcelain demitasse cups. I contemplate Mosley—compact, eager. A gap in his front teeth gives him an impish smile. There's much warmth in his soulful brown eyes. From a distance, the bartender sneezes. "Gesundheit," says Mosley.

I ask Mosley if he feels Jewish. "Sure," he says. I ask him what it means to him to be Jewish. "In a way, to be a Jew is to be a part of a tribe," he says. "Being a part of a tribe, you can never really escape your identity. You can be anything inside, but in the end you're always answerable to your blood." I ask if it's harder to be black or Jewish in America and he pauses, eyes twinkling as he ponders the question, though he has no doubt heard it often before.

"People say to me, 'Well, Walter, you're both black and white.' And I go,

'No, I'm black, and I'm Jewish. Jews are not white people.' They get mad at me. American Jews get mad at me. White people get mad at me. Black people get mad at me." He recites the line from an old Tom Lehrer lyric, "Oh, the Protestants hate the Catholics and the Catholics hate the Protestants and the Hindus hate the Muslims, and everybody hates the Jews!" Once he told an interviewer for another Jewish publication that Jews were not white people, and the magazine refused to run the story. He leans in. If this happens with *Moment*, he adds, let me know.

· · ·

MOSLEY'S MOTHER WAS ELLA SLATKIN, an intellectual Jew, whose family fled Eastern Europe in search of a utopia and came upon the promised land of California. His father Leroy Mosley was a southern storyteller, a citizen philosopher, and in his son's words "a black Socrates," who was raised in Louisiana. Like other black veterans who returned from Europe during World War II to find themselves still regarded as second-class citizens, Leroy knew there was no future for him in the South. He headed to California where he worked his way up as far as 1950s America would allow, eventually becoming a supervising custodian at a public school in Los Angeles. Ella and Leroy met while working at the school—he as a janitor, she as a clerk. Although interracial marriage was legal in California when they tried to marry in 1951, they couldn't get a license. It wasn't until after Walter was born in 1952 that the state recognized their marriage.

He was their only child. For $9.50 a week, they sent him to Victory Baptist, a private black elementary school that pioneered the teaching of African-American history long before that field's acceptance in academia. On weekends, he recalls going to the Fairfax section of Los Angeles to visit Uncle Chaim and Aunt Fanny, Uncle Abe and Cousin Louie, but he remembers few mentions of religion. "My relatives were all socialists, communists from Eastern Europe," Mosley says. "They didn't come here to go to shul, they came here to build that ideal life that people were thinking about in the late part of the 19th century." He argues that Ella went further than any of her idealistic relatives by marrying a black man, but thinks her relatives accepted the union because "they understood black life perfectly. They had lived in ghettoes and shtetls. They identified with people being hung and burned and spurned for being a different race."

The Mosleys never celebrated Passover, Rosh Hashanah or bar mitzvahs. Even secular holidays were pretty much ignored. Thanksgiving, he recalls, usually meant turkey sandwiches at the coffee shop. The marriage of Ella and Leroy was a union bred of a shared history of discrimination, a mutual conviction about the promise of a progressive future, not one steeped in ceremony. In a literal sense, Walter Mosley was the product of two traditions where the centerpiece of cultural memory was tsuris. Raised hearing stories of discrimination in the Jim Crow South and persecution in Hitler's Europe, he infuses his writing with a sense that blacks and Jews—no matter how assimilated they may feel—can be reclaimed at any moment by bigotry.

It is Mosley's conviction that like blacks, Jews are a race. He has called Jews "the Negroes of Europe," noting that even in America, Jews have long been shut out of some country clubs, professions and universities, not because their religion is different but because they are. Having adapted to their surroundings, he believes, Jews may seem white because white is the color of privilege. "One of the survival techniques of Jewish culture is to blend in to the society that you live in," he says. "If you can speak the language and do the business and wear the clothes and join the clubs, it's easier." I ask if Judaism is not more of a religion than a race. "Some people can be incredibly religious and that will trump the notion of race." But he adds with a knowing laugh, "there are very few Jews who are religious."

• • •

Mosley did not become a writer overnight. A person of the book, Ella filled her son's library card with authors like Dickens, Zola and Camus. Mosley recalls that she was not warm but believed in him and instilled in him the notion that he "was special and could do things" he "couldn't imagine." But for all their pride, his parents' ambitions for their son were modest. Ella thought he might make a good hotel manager. Leroy thought there was a career in prison work, though he advised Walter to "pay the rent and do what you love."

Mosley, part of the baby boom generation, did not seem at first to have any direction. There was what he describes as a "long-haired hippie"

phase drifting around Santa Cruz and Europe. Then a chapter at Goddard College in Vermont, where he tried to get credit for cross-country
hitchhiking before an advisor suggested that really he should drop out.
Eventually he enrolled in another school in Vermont, Johnson State College, about as far from South Central Los Angeles as he could get, where
he graduated with a degree in political science. After a brief flirtation
with grad school in political theory at the University of Minnesota, he
returned east to be with Joy Kellman, a dancer. They married in 1987,
divorced in 2001. Kellman is Jewish; Mosley chooses not to speak of their
marriage. His face looks so pained when I bring it up that I decide not to
ask him about reports that his wife's parents did not talk to their daughter
for several years after she married him.

Throughout the 1970s and 1980s, Mosley worked as a computer
programmer for Mobil, IBM and Dean Witter but also tried his hand
at various trades—making and selling pottery, collecting jade jewelry,
opening a catering business. He was making a living, paying the rent,
as his father had hoped. But he told one interviewer that during this
period he felt lost, empty.

Always a reader, in the late 1980s, he picked up Alice Walker's Pulitzer
Prize-winning novel, *The Color Purple*, and it rekindled in him an urge
to create, not in computer code but on the blank canvas of the monitor.
He enrolled in City College of New York (CCNY), attending classes at
night and studying on weekends. He took poetry writing from Bill Mat-
thews, creative writing from Frederic Tuten and fiction courses from Edna
O'Brien, the Irish writer who is known for the emotional turmoil of her
female characters. Reading his work, she told Mosley, "Walter, you're black,
Jewish, with a poor upbringing. There are riches therein."

And so, while on duty one day at Mobil, he typed out a sentence about
people on a back porch in Louisiana. "I don't know where it came from," he
has said. "I liked it. It spoke to me." The sentence read, "Hot sticky days in
southern Louisiana, the fire ants swarm." That is how Mosley began to write,
and how he writes still. "First there is a sentence. Then characters start coming in," he explains. "But the beginning is always just words in a sentence."

For one of his classes, he had written a novella featuring a man named
Ezekiel Rawlins. He flung his inaugural work toward the publishing giants

of New York. Fifteen agents rejected his work. So he returned to the library. After reading Graham Greene's screenplay, *The Third Man,* he decided to re-work the Easy Rawlins story into a mystery novel. Seeking editorial guidance, he gave the manuscript to Tuten, his CCNY advisor. Tuten was so impressed that he showed it to his own agent, Gloria Loomis, who also liked the novel, and W.W. Norton & Company published *Devil in a Blue Dress* in 1990. There was critical acclaim, but it was muted. Two more novels in the Easy Rawlins series followed—*A Red Death* in 1991 and *White Butterfly* in 1992. Then during the 1992 presidential campaign, Bill Clinton was spotted with a copy of *Devil in a Blue Dress* and later, as president, he told *The Wall Street Journal* that it was interesting "for all Americans" to see "the way it was from a black person's view…in the '40s, '50s and '60s." The endorsement helped catapult the hardworking wage earner to literary stardom. Mosley's next book, *Black Betty,* sold more than 100,000 copies. And in 1995, Denzel Washington starred as Easy in a neo-noir film version of *Devil in a Blue Dress.*

· · ·

MOSLEY IS NOT THE FIRST BLACK WRITER to portray blacks solving crimes in mystery novels. Chester Himes broke this ground, creating a detective series that featured two black cops in Harlem in the 1960s. But his New York City policemen, Coffin Ed Johnson and Gravedigger Jones, are insiders battling the mean streets on behalf of a meaner system. Mosley's black characters are outsiders, who solve the riddle despite the stubborn barrier of prejudice, besting a system stacked against them. And like the heroes of Mosley's comic book collection of more than 30,000, when they do rescue the vulnerable, they become larger than life. In outward appearance they may seem as ordinary as Clark Kent—flawed, conflicted, even weak. But by story's end, they look as powerful as Superman.

I ask Mosley if he would ever write a novel with a central Jewish character. "Not if he wasn't black," he replies. I lift an eyebrow. "Hardly anybody in America has written about black male heroes," he explains. "There are black male protagonists and black male supporting characters, but nobody else writes about black male heroes." Mosley's self-appointed job is to show these black heroes righting wrongs and protecting people, all in the name of justice, just like their white predecessors and contemporaries.

Mosley's fictional worlds are also filled with Jewish characters who, like their black brethren, are sympathetically portrayed outsiders. In his 11 Easy Rawlins novels, Easy gets help from a Jewish detective, Saul Lynx, who is married to a black woman. Lynx even takes a bullet for Easy in *Black Betty*. To some readers, Ben Dibbuk, the protagonist in Mosley's 2007 book of erotica, *Diablerie*, recalls dybbuks, the wandering spirits of the dead that invade the living in Jewish folklore. In *A Red Death*, set during the 1950s witch hunts, an FBI agent asks Rawlins to spy on the Polish-Jewish community in Los Angeles, which the agent believes to be a hotbed of godless socialist activism. And in *Fearless Jones,* also set in 1950s Los Angeles, Paris Minton—a black bookstore owner in Watts who sells public library cast-offs—is questioned by police about the death of Holocaust survivor Fanny Tannenbaum. Noting the derision in the cop's voice when he describes Fanny and her husband Sol as Jews, Paris observes, "Jew turned to nigger in my ears, and I started to dislike the cop."

In recent months, there has been a resurgence of interest in Mosley as a Jewish writer, sparked largely by Harold Heft, a former literature professor who contributed to a 1997 compendium on contemporary Jewish American novelists and noticed that Mosley had been excluded. In "Easy Call," an article for the Jewish online magazine *Tablet* published in April, Heft made the case for Mosley's inclusion in the Jewish-American literary canon, arguing that there is "a profoundly Jewish dimension" in his work. "What is a Jewish writer, and what is a Jewish theme?" Heft asked. "If a writer is unambiguously Jewish, doesn't it follow that any story he or she commits to paper contains, by definition, Jewish themes, whether that story involves bubbe telling shtetl folktales over a steaming pot of chicken soup, or a black detective in Los Angeles living in the 1950s?"

The first Mosley book Heft read was *The Man in My Basement,* a 2004 novel about an unemployed, often-drunk African-American man living in the family's 200-year-old home in Sag Harbor, New York. Charles Blakey is on the verge of losing his house when a white man, Anniston Bennet, offers to rent out the basement so he can imprison himself to atone for his sins. Downstairs, Blakey becomes a warden eliciting gruesome tales of Bennet's record of child murder while upstairs he trolls through the Blakey family archives, discovering the richness of his heritage. The book is "a hidden little gem" that would have gotten a lot more attention if it had been written by an Ishmael Reed rather than someone known for mystery novels, says Derek Maus, an associate professor of English at the State University of New York at Potsdam, co-editor of *Finding a Way Home: A Critical Assessment of Walter Mosley's Fiction.* "Mosley was a victim of his own success in what is often perceived as an unserious genre," explains Maus. For Heft, the book was an eye-opening introduction, but it was years before he learned that Mosley was Jewish. He wondered if it was a coincidence, or whether "there was something all along that was speaking to me as a Jew?"

• • •

To Mosley, the debate over whether he is or is not a Jewish author comes as no surprise. "It doesn't bother me because I understand," he told Heft last year. "You have Jewish thinkers who wouldn't include me, because they see Jews in America as white people." For his own part, he is comfortable with the identities he inherited from his parents. Even in the kitchen, the two cultures merged. "Every kind of ethnicity is great with me," he says. "If it's soul food or kreplach, I'm going to be eating it." In interviews, he talks openly about his Jewish roots. "My mother's a Jew and that makes me a Jew. That means they would take me in Israel," he told Heft.

The question of whether Mosley should be included in anthologies of Jewish authors is mirrored in black literary circles, where discussions swirl about what it means to be a "black author." Mosley's status as a best-selling author, an airport favorite, assures him a place as a mainstream writer. Perhaps that is why he disdains others' descriptions of him as a black crime writer, preferring the moniker "novelist." Even that is a restriction on his oeuvre, which also includes several nonfiction books. In 2003, on the second anniversary of the September 11 terrorist attacks, he published *What Next: A Memoir Toward World Peace,* arguing that African Americans are the only believable American ambassadors for world peace. "We know what the rest of the world feels about American rhetoric on democracy because we have been lied to about freedom and carry a similar rage in our hearts," he wrote. This was followed by his 2005 epistle, *Life Out of Context,* in which he called for the creation of a black party to challenge the stranglehold of the United States' two-party system. His first play, *The Fall of Heaven,* based on his 2008 book, *The Tempest Tales*, which tackles questions of good and evil, premiered at the Cincinnati Playhouse in the Park this year.

Mosley's literary output has evolved with the times. Easy, a figure of Leroy Mosley's generation, serves as a bridge between two separate and unequal worlds. "Easy Rawlins, every door he walked through he knew what he was going to find on the other side," says Mosley. Easy could be surprised "by character, by beauty, by ugliness, by crime…but you know when you walk through a black neighborhood or a white neighborhood, you know pretty much what's going to happen." Leonid McGill, the hero of Mosley's latest mystery series, of which this year's *Known to Evil* is the second installment, "never knows" what he will discover behind a closed door. Leonid is a figure of the Obama age, when what Mosley dubs a "meta-racial" society elected a black man to the presidency.

Still, he bristles at the suggestion that American society has entered into a post-racial period and has matured beyond the evil legacies of slavery and segregation. "He is distrustful of the idea that we've moved on," says Derek Maus. "He understands the raisin in the batter metaphor. No matter how much you stir, you cannot assimilate the raisin into the batter." Mosley clings proudly to the role of outsider, a view that derives as much from class as color. "I doubt he will ever write about somebody of privilege as a hero figure," says Maus. Rarely are Mosley's Jewish characters assimilated or wealthy. "He identifies with European Jews, with camp survivors. There is this linkage to old European Jewishness."

Back at Dish, Mosley clasps a finger, adorned with a ring from his nephrite jade collection, around his espresso cup as I return to the uncomfortable question of comparative discrimination. He deftly avoids it, declining to say which history hurts the most—the social memory of chains and degradations of whippings, rapes and being wrenched from your family because you were property, or the inhumanity of being marched off to concentration camps to face starvation, forced labor, humiliation and near-certain death. "Comparing holocausts doesn't seem a plausible thing to me," he says. "You look at women in the Congo today and you say, 'I don't know what's harder, being black or being Jewish, but I'll take either one as long as I don't have to be a woman in the Congo.'" ◐

7

BOB DYLAN: THE
UNAUTHORIZED SPIRITUAL BIOGRAPHY

Nadine Epstein & Rebecca Frankel • *August/September 2005*

IN THE EARLY 1960s, Bob Dylan performed at tiny Greenwich Village folk clubs, acoustic guitar strapped across his compact shoulders, harmonica perched on a metal rack around his slender neck. His chord changes were simple and his voice a soft-grating croon. With lyrics that were eerily profound, the Midwestern folksinger soon found himself labeled a "prophet" of his generation.

The young musician's fans were spiritual, not religious in the traditional sense; many were abandoning the churches and synagogues of their parents in search of something new. But even those Jews who felt little connection with Judaism could not suppress a hint of pride as they listened to songs like "Blowin' in the Wind" and "The Times They Are A-Changin'," anthems that were reverently taken up by other 1960s legends like Judy Collins, *The Byrds* and *Peter, Paul & Mary*. Bob Dylan, the poet of their generation, was Jewish.

Those young Jews who worshiped in the Temple of Dylan never wanted him to be anything other than what he was: a musical troubadour preaching his own brand of spirituality. They couldn't have foreseen the day, nearly two decades later, when Dylan would come forward as a man reborn, singing his love for a Christian savior. "Are you ready to meet Jesus?" asked a song on his 1980 album *Saved*. "Are you where you ought to be?/Will He know you when He sees you/or will He say, 'Depart from Me?'"

Jesus long ago vanished from Dylan's lyrical vocabulary. At 64, he wears a gentlemanly cowboy hat in place of the corduroy cap from his Greenwich Village days, and lines now gather around his blue eyes. Yet, as he continues to crisscross the world on his Never-Ending Tour, he remains as much of an enigma as ever.

After decades of wondering about his religious identity, *Moment* takes a look back at Dylan's spiritual journey. We begin in Hibbing, the small Midwestern mining town where Bob Dylan once lived, back when they called him Bobby Zimmerman…

· · ·

U.S. 50 IS LINED WITH the still-bare trees of early April blending with the evergreen spruces and jack pines. Past the rolling Minnesota hills, corrals of horses and cattle give way to hints of commercial life. Motels and fast food joints common to any Midwest highway flash by. A small sign appears ahead. "Hibbing" it says in large, white letters, "20 Miles."

Like other small cities, Hibbing has its claims to fame. Built on Minnesota's Mesabi Iron Range in the 1890s, it boasts a six-mile by three-mile, 500-foot-deep gash in the earth—the Hull-Rust Mahoney mine—the world's largest open-air mine. It's also the birthplace of baseball great Roger Maris, Boston Celtics legend Kevin McHale and the once-mighty American company known as Greyhound Bus.

Soon enough you've passed the mile stretch of modest homes and are heading west on the handsome main drag—Howard Street—into downtown Hibbing, six or so blocks of turn-of-the-century brick buildings interspersed with newer structures. Many are vacant or underused, but during World War II, when demand for iron was at its peak, businesses here prospered. Most were owned and run by Jewish immigrants from Eastern Europe who had come to stay with landsmen until they could get on their feet. They stayed on, despite the fact that they were isolated from most of their American Jewish brethren, and became the vital center of the town's commercial life.

By the 1970s, most of these businesses were gone. "When the mine closed and the miners lost their jobs, people were forced to move, and so the Jews who owned the stores lost their customers," says Steve Jolowsky, 45. One of the handful of Jews remaining in Hibbing, Jolowsky runs his family's scrap yard.

Hibbing's downtown stands as a monument to its once-vibrant Jewish community. "Every single store except for the J.C. Penney's was owned by Jews," recalls Neil Schwartz, 53, who grew up in Hibbing and is now a cantor in Chattanooga, Tennessee. A glance at the 1942 Hibbing City

Directory confirms this observation: Hyman Bloom owned the Boston Department Store, Jacob Jowolsky operated Hibbing Auto Wrecking. Nathan Nides owned Nides Fashion Shop, sold insurance and lent money. The First Avenue Market was owned by David Shapiro, Jack and Israel Sher ran the Insurance Service Agency and Louis Stein was the proprietor of Stein's Drug Store. The Edelstein-Stones owned a string of movie palaces, including the local drive-in and the Lybba Theater on Howard Street, named after Bob Dylan's maternal great-grandmother Lybba Edelstein, who came to the United States from Lithuania in 1902.

On May 24, 1941, 10-pound Robert "Bobby" Allen was born to Abe Zimmerman and his wife Beatrice "Beatty" at St. Mary's Hospital in Duluth. Beatty had grown up in Hibbing, 86 miles to the northwest. Abe was the son of Zigman and Anna Zimmerman, Jewish immigrants from Odessa.

Bobby's bris was held in the Zimmermans' apartment in the largely Jewish central hillside district of Duluth, where Abe managed the stock department for Standard Oil. When Bobby was six, Abe, an avid athlete, fell ill with polio and was left with a weak leg that made walking painful. The family moved to Hibbing where Abe went into business with his brothers Maurice and Paul, who owned and operated an electric supply, appliance and furniture store.

The home the Zimmerman family eventually settled into (another son, David, soon came along) is easy to find. Its photo is posted on the Hibbing website along with its street number, 2425 Seventh Avenue East. The two-story, boxy, blue stucco house has a maroon-red door. Three smartly trimmed bushes flank the walk to the front steps. Seventh Avenue is wide with little traffic. It is lined with trees and small houses, some with porches, and seems steeped in generations of quiet and calm. It is all very ordinary.

It was here that Bobby Zimmerman grew up, surrounded by a loving family and a stable Jewish community that numbered nearly 300. There was nothing exceptional about his childhood. His father was president of B'nai Brith, and his mother was president of Hadassah.

Beatty, says Robert Shelton in his 1986 biography of Dylan entitled *No Direction Home*, was a "bubbly woman, blond, headstrong, nervous, volatile and warm." Abe was "a short man with an appealing smile," who was more often than not seen with a cigar. Their home was "clean and orderly" and "always ready for a visit." They were the kind of parents who would read and re-read the Mother's and Father's Day poems penned by their not-yet-famous son, pulling them from a drawer to share with visitors.

Bobby attended religious school at Agudas Achim, the community's only synagogue. "Bob was a rambunctious but nice kid," religious school principal Shirley Schwartz told her son Neil, the Tennessee cantor. In the summers, Bobby attended Herzl Camp, a popular Zionist camp in northwestern Wisconsin, where he swam and boated, learned Hebrew and played piano, guitar and harmonica with his fellow campers.

When Bobby came of age, 400 people attended his bar mitzvah party—rumored to be the largest ever held in Hibbing—at the city's grand Androy Hotel. Bobby had prepared for his Torah and Haftorah readings with Reuben Maier, an Orthodox rabbi from Brooklyn. They studied in an apartment at 419 East Howard, right above the L&B Café, which had the best jukebox in town. The rabbi's arrival in Hibbing was, according to Dylan in a 1985 interview with *Spin*, serendipitous.

"The town didn't have a rabbi…He showed up just in time for me to learn this stuff. He was an old man…with a white beard and wore a black hat and black clothes. They put him upstairs of the café, which was the local hangout. It was a rock 'n' roll café where I used to hang out, too. I used to go up there every day to learn this stuff, either after school or after dinner. After studying with him an hour or so, I'd come down and boogie. The rabbi taught me what I had to learn and after he conducted the bar mitzvah, he just disappeared…I never saw him again…He came and went like a ghost."

In the same interview, Dylan went on to say that he believed Rabbi Maier was forced out of the community because he was Orthodox, and too different from the more assimilated Jews of Hibbing. "Jews separate themselves like that. Orthodox, Conservative, Reform, as if God calls them that. Christians, too. Baptists…Methodists, Calvinists. God has no respect for a person's title. He don't care what you call yourself."

The tone of Dylan's recollection may give a hint of what it was like to be a Jew in a town dominated by descendants of the great Scandinavian immigration about whom Garrison Keillor, that other American poet from Minnesota, so fondly spins tales. A teacher at Hibbing High told biographer Robert Shelton that while many barriers had been razed, some remained.

"In Hibbing, the Finns hated the Bohemians and the Bohemians hated the Finns. Nearly everyone hated the Jews." According to Shelton, one of Dylan's classmates said, "The kids used to tease Bob, sometimes. They would call him Bobby Zennerman because it was so difficult to pronounce Zimmerman. He didn't like that…His feelings could be hurt easily. Later in high school he wasn't so well liked, mostly because he stayed to himself so much."

"All I did was write and sing…dissolve myself into situations where I was invisible," Dylan said of his teenage years, when he hid away in his family's attached garage with rock bands called *The Shadow Blasters* and *The Golden Chords*. Shelton connects this need for invisibility to the struggles of what he called alien assimilation. "The thirty or forty Jewish families of Hibbing still had to huddle together against the cold. Abe, who loved to play golf, couldn't belong to the Masabi Country Club."

A grandchild of immigrants, Bobby nevertheless was very American. He attended public school, where he did well when he wanted to, and had non-Jewish friends including girlfriend Echo Hellstrom. It's quite possible that his sense of social justice was honed by the Hibbing miner strikes of 1949 and 1952. And his taste in music was heavily influenced by the energetic sounds of Little Richard and the 1950s rock 'n' roll he picked up at night on his AM radio. He liked to emulate his favorite rebel, James Dean; when he performed at his high school talent show, the quiet Zimmerman surprised many with his rocking music, irritating the principal and delighting his peers.

In the fall of 1959, when Hibbing's Jewish population had dropped to 155, Bobby Zimmerman set off for college, leaving his family and small-town Judaism behind. In this way, he was no different from thousands of young Jews throughout the Midwest: they were all part of the same downward spiral that eventually led Hibbing's stores and theaters to close and Agudas Achim to be shuttered and sold as a private home. Merchants' children left because they didn't want the businesses, in part because they were waning, and in part because their hometowns offered few opportunities.

Bobby enrolled at the University of Minnesota in Minneapolis, where it is said that he considered joining a Jewish fraternity before declaring it meaningless. But much to his father's dismay, he preferred performing at coffee houses to schoolwork, and adopted the decidedly non-Semitic sounding name Bob Dylan.

• • •

LATE IN 1960 HE HEADED for Greenwich Village. His arrival was well timed. This talented and driven young man came into a world on the cusp of change populated by Beat poets and folk singers, influenced by Woody Guthrie (Dylan regularly visited Guthrie—who had married a Jewish woman and was fascinated by all things Jewish—as he lay ailing in a hospital), Leadbelly and Pete Seeger—three Dylan idols who had been recorded by Moses Asch, the founder of Folkways Records and son of the great Yiddish writer, Sholem Asch. Rock 'n' roll was about to join forces with massive political activism and give birth to a new generation of American music.

Dylan hung out at small clubs, absorbing the scene in what some call his "sponge" period. As he writes in his 2004 *Chronicles, Volume One*, the old folk songs in his early repertoire were his "preceptor and guide into some altered consciousness of reality, some different republic, some liberated republic." He later describes some of the folk and blues concerts he attended when he first came to New York as "spiritual experiences…I wasn't ready to act on it but knew somehow, though, that if I wanted to stay playing music, that I would have to claim a larger part of myself."

"Being a musician means…getting to the depths of where you are at," Dylan told *Playboy* in 1966. "And most any musician would try anything to get to those depths, because playing music is an immediate thing…Your spirit flies when you are playing music. So with music, you tend to look deeper and deeper inside yourself to find the music."

By the end of the 1960s, Dylan had turned popular music on its head, says Scott R. Benarde, author of the book, *Stars of David: Rock 'n' Roll's Jewish Stories*. "He bent and broke songwriting rules, contemplating God, morality and justice in songs as few had done, inspired, if not invented, the musical form of folk rock…recorded folk, blues, country rock…defying those who would label him, and irritated fans by rendering his classic songs unrecognizable in concert. Through it all he never looked back."

Dylan was a spiritual seeker at the dawn of a new era and he poured his yearnings into his music. He was heavily influenced by gospel and bluegrass, both outgrowths of the country's Christian roots. His lyrics, like those of his musical heroes, were laden with biblical imagery.

The title song from Dylan's 1965 album *Highway 61 Revisited* opens with a direct allusion to the Torah: "Oh God said to Abraham, 'Kill me a son'/Abe says, 'Man, you must be puttin' me on'/God say 'No.' Abe say, 'What?'/God say, 'You can do what you want Abe, but/The next time you see me comin' you better run'/'Well,' Abe says, 'Where do you want this killin' done?'/ God says, 'Out on Highway 61.'"

Despite the recurrence of Jewish themes in his work, Dylan was not easy to read. He was famously coy and often evasive while giving interviews, and he was particularly contradictory when speaking about religion. This made it easy for fans to invest his lyrics with their own meaning, says Ron Rosenbaum, discussing his 1978 *Playboy* interview with Dylan. "At times he spoke like a prophet with that elliptical logic reminiscent of the biblical teachers, and that same sense of cutting to the core meaning of things."

Some of Dylan's lyrics reflected an ongoing struggle with religion that bordered on the existential. "When the Second World War/Came to an end/We forgave the Germans/And we were friends/Though they murdered six million/In the ovens they fried/The Germans now too/Have God on their side," he wrote in "With God On Our Side" on his 1963 album *The Times They Are A-Changin'*.

Dylan was hungry for knowledge and willing to redefine himself spiritually in order to find it. "Got no religion," Dylan would tell Izzy Young in 1961. Young was the owner of the Folklore Center, the hub for Village folk musicians. "Tried a bunch of different religions. The churches are divided. Can't make up their minds, and neither can I. Never saw a god; can't say until I see one." Later, in his 1966 interview with *Playboy*, Dylan said that he had never really felt Jewish. "I don't really consider myself Jewish or non-Jewish...I'm not a patriot to any creed. I believe in all of them and none of them."

But if Dylan evaded religious labels he wasn't afraid to challenge the agnosticism that was prevalent among 1960s intellectuals. "I remember seeing a *TIME* magazine cover on an airplane a few years back and it had a big cover headline, 'IS GOD DEAD?'" Dylan told *Playboy*. "I mean, that was—would you think that was a responsible thing to do? What does God think of that? I mean, if you were God, how would you like to see that written about yourself? You know, I think the country has gone downhill since that day."

By 1966, the young man from Hibbing was battling the pressures of success. When a motorcycle accident left him with a concussion and cracked vertebrae, he decided it was time to take a break from celebrity life. "I was pretty wound up before that accident," he told *Spin* in 1985. "I wasn't seeing anything in any kind of perspective. I probably would have died if I had kept on going that way."

He had married model and former Playboy Bunny Sara Lowndes (the former Shirley Nozinsky) in a civil ceremony in 1965. They settled into a very private life in Woodstock, New York. Dylan adopted Maria, Lowndes' daughter, and the couple had four more children: Jesse, Sam, Jakob and Anna.

During this period Dylan released several albums, some more critically acclaimed than others. His spiritual "I Shall be Released," recorded in 1967, may have reflected Dylan's relief at being out of the spotlight, suggests Larry Yudelson author of the article "Tangled Up in Jews," which was published in *Washington Jewish Week* in 1991. Certainly, the lyrics could lead one to that conclusion: "I see the light come shining/from the west down to the east/Any day now, Any way now/I shall be released."

The song "Forever Young" on the 1974 album *Planet Waves* may have been written for the couple's youngest son, Jakob. Scott R. Benarde notes that it is based on the parents' Blessing of the Children on Shabbat. The blessing begins: "May God bless you and keep you." Dylan's song opens with "May God bless you and keep you always/May your wishes all come true/May you always do for others/And let others do for you."

On his 30th birthday, Dylan was in Israel. According to biographer Robert Shelton, he visited a Jerusalem yeshiva where several American students asked him why he avoided talking about his Jewish identity. Shelton says that Dylan responded, "I'm a Jew. It touches my poetry, my life in ways I can't describe. Why should I declare something so obvious?"

Another intriguing Jewish connection from this period involves Norman Raeben, the son of noted writer Sholom Aleichem. Raeben was Dylan's art teacher in 1974 and his lessons are said to have inspired Dylan's painfully honest "Tangled Up in Blue."

"Norman Raeben taught me how to see...in a way that allowed me to do consciously what I unconsciously felt," Dylan writes in 1978. "And I didn't know how to pull it off. I wasn't sure it could be done in songs because I'd never written a song like that. But when I started doing it, the first album I made was *Blood on The Tracks*. Everybody agrees that it was pretty different, and what's different about it is there's a code in the lyrics and also there's no sense of time." He went on to explain that this artistic renaissance had come at a price: once he learned to refocus his energies on what he did best, his wife ceased to understand him.

By 1977, the peaceful period in Dylan's life had come to an end. His breakup with Sara, memorialized in *Blood on the Tracks*, was followed by an ugly custody battle over their children. Then Dylan made a move that few have forgotten to this day. It was touched off by a mystical experience.

"Jesus put his hand on me," he explained to Karen Hughes in 1980 in an interview later published in the New Zealand newspaper *The Dominion*. "It was a physical thing. I felt it. I felt it all over me. I felt my whole body tremble. The glory of the Lord knocked me down and picked me up...I guess He's always been calling me."

Not since Shabbatai Tzvi's 17th-century about-face had an exit from Judaism shocked the tribe like Dylan's Christian period. While he was just one of many seekers who turned to born-again Christianity during the 1970s—becoming what was then known as a Jesus Freak—it came as quite a surprise when the quintessential individualist accepted Jesus as the Ultimate Authority.

Dylan's mystical experience led him to spend time with a southern California Christian group called the Vineyard Fellowship and eventually to accept Jesus, says *Stars of David* author Benarde. Shortly after, Dylan recorded his first Christian album *Slow Train Coming*. The title song became a top 40 hit and won Dylan a Grammy for Best Male Rock Performer in 1980. His low-down "Gotta Serve Somebody" (meaning Jesus) also got lots of radio play, says Benarde. His album *Saved* disappointed fans, although the 1981 *Shot of Love* restored some of his popularity.

Throughout this period, Dylan sang his Christian songs and talked of Jesus at concerts. His public embrace of Christianity left his fans perplexed. Jews were especially uncomfortable. "I remember how disgusted my mother was," says Hibbing's Steve Jolowsky. Cantor Schwartz recalls that Dylan's conversion "certainly was a topic of discussion in whatever Jewish community I was a member of." But he adds, "Those of us that came from the hinterlands like he did predicted that it wasn't going to last, and we were right."

Dylan's mother Beatty, who died in 2000, weighed in on the subject during a 1985 interview now posted at jewhoo.com. Asked about her son's Christian period, she said, "He never displayed it for me," adding that "what religion a person is shouldn't make any difference to anybody else. I'm not bigoted in any way. Rabbis would call me up. I'd say if you're upset, you try to change him.'"

After a few years Dylan stopped spreading the word and began to distance himself from Christianity. In 1983 he traveled to Israel for his son Jesse's bar mitzvah and an Israeli photographer caught Dylan wearing tefillin and praying at the Western Wall. His album *Infidels*, which was released that same year, includes an ode to Israel called "Neighborhood Bully." Dylan, says Benarde, "uses the song to make an impassioned defense of the Jewish homeland. He illustrates how Israel (never named in the song but quite obvious), vastly outnumbered and surrounded by a hostile world, still is tagged as the region's 'neighborhood bully' for the mere act of surviving. Casting Israel," Benarde adds, "as the 'neighborhood bully' is exactly what the Palestinians have managed to do two and a half decades after Dylan wrote the song."

"The neighborhood bully just lives to survive/He's criticized and condemned for being alive/He's not supposed to fight back/He's supposed to have thick skin/He's supposed to lay down and die when his door is kicked in/He's the neighborhood bully."

By this time, according to "Tangled Up in Jews" author Larry Yudelson, Jesus had vanished from Dylan's lyrical vocabulary, replaced by "the books of Leviticus and Deuteronomy." Yudelson reports that Dylan told an interviewer about his born-again period: "[It] was all part of my experience. It had to happen. When I get involved in something, I get totally involved. I don't just play around the fringes."

In the years that followed, there were many Dylan sightings in Jewish venues including Chabad telethons, during one of which he is reported to have said, "Chabad is my favorite organization in the whole world, really." According to a 1986 article by Mike Santangelo in *The Daily News*, Dylan spent several years in the 1980s studying with the Lubavitcher Jews of Brooklyn, receiving instruction from Talmudic scholars and listening to tapes of Rebbe Menachem Schneerson. Since then he has been seen praying with Chabad in Los Angeles, Minneapolis-St. Paul and New York.

Dylan is now patriarch of a large and mostly Jewish family, though exact details are not publicly known. In his recent *Down the Highway: The Life of Bob Dylan*, biographer Howard Sounes revealed that Dylan secretly married gospel-rock singer Carol Dennis in 1986. They had a daughter and divorced in 1992.

In the late 1980s, Dylan's eldest daughter, Maria, a lawyer, married Peter Himmelman, a well-known and talented musician. Himmelman, who grew up in Minnesota, discovered Chabad as a young man, and the couple has chosen to send their four children to Jewish day schools near their home in Santa Monica, California.

Dylan's eldest son Jesse may also be observant, and his youngest son, Jakob, now 35 and frontman for the critically acclaimed band, *The Wallflowers*, has spoken publicly about his Jewishness. "I am Jewish and that's what's there," the young Dylan told Mick Brown of *The Daily Telegraph* in 2000. In an article in *Details*, Jakob said that he and his brothers came by their biblical names because of their parents' interest in Judaism. A few months ago, in an interview with Anthony DeCurtis in *The New York Times*, just before *The Wallflowers* released their new album (on May 24th, Bob Dylan's 64th birthday), Jakob reveals what it was like to grow up with a famous father. "Do most kids have people crash their bar mitzvah?" he asks.

· · ·

WHEN NIGHTTIME FALLS IN HIBBING, the quiet settles even deeper. Few establishments are open for business and the words of one former visitor come to mind: "Hibbing by night is any small town on the edge of nowhere."

Zimmy's Bar and Grill is usually the first stop for those Dylan pilgrims who make it to Hibbing. The door and awning of the brick-square restaurant are mismatched shades of red, and the predictable Dylan memorabilia hangs on the walls. A few locals sit at the bar.

"It's pretty easy to spot out-of-towners on a Dylan quest because they usually come in alone," says co-owner Linda Stroback-Hocking, who moved to Hibbing from Philadelphia and is a huge Dylan fan. Once they arrive, the Dylan seekers study the decor, buy T-shirts and shot glasses, and order Hard Rain Hamburgers and Hurricane Carter Reuben sandwiches.

Nearly 45 years after Dylan left Hibbing, he plays on, so busy performing in the out-of-the-way venues he prefers that he can't have much time for the homes he keeps in Minnesota, California and New York, let alone his boat in the Caribbean. All that really can be said is that he remains true to himself. The man known for making statements that are out of step with logic that he has presented earlier remains consistent in his devotion to self-discovery.

Perhaps the time has come for his Jewish fans to forgive Robert Zimmerman for his brief sojourn away from the faith. Many ardent Jewish Dylan admirers believe that he had to leave Judaism in order to return more fully. Scott R. Benarde suggests that we "consider Dylan's fling with Christianity his moment of Yisrael, of 'wrestling with God.'"

A friend who knows Bob Dylan well, and who wishes to remain anonymous, offers this: "Being Jewish and being connected to G-d in the traditional Jewish way is an important part of who Bob is. He knows his talent and success are gifts that have been given to him by G-d. When it is Bob's time to be called back to his creator, Jewish people, family, friends and fans will say Kaddish for him according to the Jewish tradition. And it will be good, and his soul will be happy." ✿

8

BRIAN EPSTEIN: THE
MAN BEHIND THE BEATLES

Nadine Epstein & Walter J. Podrazik • *August/September 2006*

During his lunch break on November 9, 1961, Brian Epstein—the 27-year-old Jewish proprietor of Liverpool's popular North End Music Store—walked the 250 steps from his shop, through an alley and down the 18 stone stairs to a local cellar club appropriately called the Cavern.

Passionate about classical and Broadway music, Epstein had paid little attention to the city's burgeoning teenage beat scene until, as legend has it, October 28th. A customer named Raymond Jones came into his shop asking for the single "My Bonnie," by a band called *The Beatles*. A few days later, a gaggle of girls made the same request. Epstein was puzzled: There was no such record available from any British label. After some digging, he'd found that the record had been issued in Germany. The band was not credited anywhere on the disc but it was available as an import. He was surprised to discover that the group was from Liverpool and was, coincidentally, playing at a nearby club on Mathew Street.

When Epstein and his assistant Alistair Taylor arrived at the Cavern that day, they were the oldest guests and certainly the only ones in suits. The lunchtime show had drawn in a flood of scruffy teenagers. As Epstein wrote in his 1964 autobiography, *A Cellarful of Noise*, the atmosphere was not at all to his liking. "Inside the club it was black and deep as a grave and I regretted my decision to come."

The band—John Lennon, Paul McCartney, George Harrison and then drummer Pete Best—were wearing black leather jackets, their hair wild and unkempt. Epstein was intrigued by what he heard but, trained in theater and fastidious in his own appearance, he was put off by the band's primitive stage habits. "They smoked as they played, and they ate, and pretended to hit each other…But they gave a captivating and honest show and they had very considerable magnetism. I loved their ad libs and was fascinated by this, to me, new music with its pounding bass beat and vast engulfing sound."

During a break, Epstein poked his head into the tiny room next to the stage, introduced himself and Taylor, and complimented the band. Harrison looked up and smiled. "Hello there," he said dryly. "What brings Mr. Epstein here?" Harrison called over his band mates, all of whom were delighted that Epstein had enjoyed the music. They recognized him from the record shop, where they liked to hang out between gigs.

Epstein invited the band members to his shop on Whitechapel Street for a "chat" on December 3rd. In the intervening weeks, he sold over 100 copies of "My Bonnie." When *The Beatles* arrived, Epstein announced in his soft-spoken way: "Quite simply, you need a manager. Would you like me to do it?"

While Epstein had no experience as a band manager, he had the intuition of a natural businessman. He sensed that the appeal the boys possessed had enormous potential. *The Beatles* were thrilled when he offered his services. He promised to secure higher performance fees for their shows, extricate them from their German record contract and sign them with a British label. The young men were particularly impressed when Epstein assured them that he would not interfere with their music. Impatient for success outside Liverpool, it was Lennon who was the first to commit: "Right then, Brian, manage us. Where's the contract? I'll sign it."

Epstein was only six years older than Lennon, the band's self-styled leader, but to *The Beatles*, young men from the working class, Epstein was from a different world. The Epstein family was one of the most prominent Jewish families in Liverpool, residing in the genteel suburb of Childwall where, it's been said, "doors had silver letterboxes and a ding-dong bell would chime and an aproned maid would answer it." Elegant with his swank accent, Epstein wore pinstriped suits with silk cravats and drove a luxury Zephyr Zodiac. "We thought he was some very posh rich fellow," Harrison said in the 1995 documentary *The Beatles Anthology*. To Lennon, "He looked efficient and rich," and, McCartney: "We were very impressed by anyone in a suit or with a car."

Some of their parents weren't so easily won over. "Olive Johnson, the

McCartney family's close friend, received a call from [Jim] McCartney in a state of some anxiety over his son's proposed association with a 'Jew-boy,'" according to Philip Norman's 1981 biography, *SHOUT! The Beatles in Their Generation.*

Epstein met with each family individually, and soon the parents were as pleased as their sons. "My Dad, when he heard about Brian wanting to manage us, said, 'This could be a very good thing,'" McCartney said in an interview with producer Debbie Geller for a 1998 BBC documentary called *The Brian Epstein Story.* "He thought Jewish people were very good with money. This was the common wisdom. Dad thought Brian would be very good for us. He thought Brian was very sensible, very charming. He was right."

* * *

BRIAN SAMUEL EPSTEIN was born on September 19, 1934, on Yom Kippur to Harry Epstein and Malkah "Queenie" Hyman. (Malkah means queen in Hebrew.) Two years later, Queenie gave birth to another son, Clive. By all accounts, the Epsteins had a loving home. "It looked in those days that the Epsteins were a golden family, quite like a fairy story," Harry's sister Stella Carter once mused.

Harry and Queenie were both children of Jewish immigrants from Eastern Europe. Harry worked with his father, Isaac, in the family's I. Epstein & Son. It was a lucrative business and the Epstein house at 197 Queens Drive in Childwall was spacious and comfortable, with a front lawn, a back garden and a garage. Inside there was rich wood paneling, stained glass, two bathrooms and five bedrooms, each with a mezuzah on the doorpost.

Although Harry kept the store open on Saturdays, the Epstein family was observant. "On Friday nights she [Queenie] lit the Sabbath candles and Harry said prayers," wrote the late Ray Coleman, author of the 1989 biography *Brian Epstein: The Man Who Made The Beatles,* who interviewed Queenie before her death in 1997. "In the kitchen, the milk and meat dishes were separated, as were the cutlery and crockery. Jewish dietary rules were observed."

The Epsteins were members of an Orthodox shul—Greenbank Drive Hebrew Congregation—where Brian and Clive attended cheder on Sundays for religious studies and to learn Hebrew. When it was discovered that

Epstein had been taught the wrong parsha for his bar mitzvah, he quickly mastered the new one. "He was obviously well educated in Hebrew and Hebrew liturgy," an uncle told Debbie Geller, who, in 2000, also published *In My Life: The Brian Epstein Story,* a collection of interviews about Epstein. After the bar mitzvah a reception was held at the house with over one hundred guests. As a gift, Harry enrolled Brian as a synagogue member in his own right, and later did the same for Clive.

Michael Swerdlow, who belonged to the congregation, says that he admired the smartly dressed Epstein men when they arrived at services: "I recall Harry Epstein attending on high holy days and being followed into the synagogue by Brian and Clive, wearing bowler hats, which was quite fashionable for British synagogue-goers to wear."

Harry Epstein helped support the synagogue, and the family's reputation was one of financial and social solidity. "Whenever I saw the Epstein family, they looked just like a very Jewish family, the kind I would see in the Bronx or Miami Beach," recalls Nat Weiss, who was later to become one of Brian Epstein's closest friends and a business partner. "Their values were very Jewish."

• • •

Unfortunately for Epstein—who preferred the arts to sports and academics—much of his childhood was not spent in Childwall but in expensive single-sex boarding schools that children of his class were expected to attend.

At age ten, he enrolled at the prestigious Liverpool College. "Brian was rapidly convinced that there was an anti-Semitic strain running through it," wrote Coleman. The school insisted that Brian attend school activities on Saturday mornings, which prevented him from going to synagogue with his father. Another Jew who studied at Liverpool College, Brian Wolfson, has said that the culture of the school wasn't anti-Semitic, but "there were 600 boys, a half dozen Catholics and 25 Jews. Life wasn't easy," especially for a sensitive boy like Epstein.

Later, Queenie and Harry decided to send him to Beaconsfeld School, a Jewish boarding school. "This I enjoyed a little better and I took up horse-riding and art, both of which I did pretty well," Epstein recalled in his autobiography. "I began to feel more at evens with the world and I made friends with a horse called Amber, who got on very well with Jews and didn't care that I'd been expelled from Liverpool College."

Epstein flourished in acting and painting, and at one time wanted to be a dress designer, a calling his parents discouraged. With mediocre grades, however, he couldn't get into a top school like Eton, and attended what was called a "minor" public school. "Naturally, my first term at public school was slightly marred by the ragging—being a Jew and not showing a great keenness for sports, the boys had good enough reason for my persecution," Epstein wrote.

His school experience left an indelible mark on his psyche, according to Rex Makin, a Queens Drive neighbor. Makin—president of the Stapley Home for Aged Jews in Liverpool while Harry was treasurer—told Geller he believed that these anti-Semitic experiences at school left Epstein ambivalent about religion and gave him "an inferiority complex." But Epstein would emerge from his formative years with a perspective on life that set him apart from most Liverpudlians. As Geller observes, being Jewish was an important factor in Epstein's makeup. "It meant he was an outsider who appreciated the importance of transcending society's view."

Life on the stage was Epstein's dream but he was destined for the family business. "I am the elder son—a hallowed position in a Jewish family—and much was to be expected of me," he wrote. "My father…naturally sought in me some sign of an adequate heir to the family business, but alas, he scarcely saw a sign of any quality at all beyond a loyalty to the family, which, thanks to the steadfastness of my parents, has never faltered."

In 1950, at age sixteen, Epstein dropped out of school to join his grandfather and father at the store on Walton Road in Liverpool. I. Epstein & Son was a proper, even stuffy establishment that outfitted households throughout the region. Young Epstein brought a fresh eye to the business that at first may have aggravated his grandfather but, as it turned out, he had quite a talent for display work and interior decorating, making him an ideal furniture salesman. Epstein possessed a reassuring and persuasive manner that convinced customers to "trade up" in quality and quantity.

At eighteen, Epstein was called up for the mandatory two years of National Service in the British military. It was a miserable experience for him.

Although he excelled at clerical duties, he was a disaster in field situations. He hated the regimentation of army life, but was disappointed he hadn't been promoted beyond the rank of private. After returning to his barracks in London's Regent's Park one evening dressed in his normal civilian attire—suit, bowler hat and umbrella—Epstein was mistaken for an officer and found himself facing a trumped-up charge of impersonating one. The army sent him to several psychiatrists and finally came to the conclusion that he just wasn't soldier material. Epstein was relieved when he was given a medical discharge in January 1954.

Back in Liverpool, he worked at the furniture store by day and enjoyed the life of a bon vivant by night. He and his childhood friend Joe Flannery loved to go to the theater and see music shows, except on Friday nights when Epstein joined his parents and brother for Shabbat dinner. "One time Vivien Leigh came to Liverpool to play at the Royal Court for two weeks in *A Streetcar Named Desire*, and we booked the same two seats for every night," Flannery says. "On the Friday night Brian wasn't with me and Vivien Leigh took the trouble to put her foot through the footlights and lean over the stage and ask, 'Where is your friend tonight?' I said, 'It's Friday night and you should know,' and she said, 'Yes, that's right.'"

"Brian had no qualms about being Jewish," says Flannery, who knew the Epsteins well. Though Flannery was raised Catholic, Harry Epstein used to teasingly call him "Yossel," Yiddish for Joseph. He and Epstein would meet for lunch regularly as Flannery worked at his own family's store just down the street from I. Epstein & Son.

The two friends had long talks and sometimes discussed Epstein's sexual attraction to men. In an era during which homosexual behavior was not just controversial but illegal in England, the young man was tortured by his feelings and the situations in which he found himself. In those years gay relationships had to be cloaked in secrecy, especially in Liverpool, explains Flannery.

"It was after the army that I found out about the existence of the various rendezvous and homosexual 'life,'" Geller quotes from Epstein's diaries. His predicament was made worse by the fact that he gravitated to a rough crowd. On more than one occasion he was involved in scuffles that left him bruised and bleeding. "All the time that I knew him, I don't think one could say that he ever had any proper long-term emotional relationship,"

Flannery says. "The people he was attracted to were not the kind of people you settle down with. He wasn't comfortable about the fact that he was gay and, therefore, that led to a situation where he couldn't have a successful homosexual relationship. That inability came from the fact that being gay was not his ideal way of living his life, subconscious, as that may have been. I don't think that was unusual for his time."

Epstein's homosexuality added another dimension to his Jewish sensibility of being an outsider. "At no time did he want to be notorious for being gay," says Weiss. "It wasn't a crime to be a Jew. But it was a crime to be a homosexual."

Life in Liverpool became stifling. In 1956, Epstein convinced his father to give him leave from the business to attend the Royal Academy of Dramatic Art (RADA) in London. His contemporaries included such performers as Susannah York, Peter Blythe, Peter O'Toole, Albert Finney and Joanna Dunham. While Epstein was a respectable actor, he realized that he would never advance beyond secondary roles. He did not return for the fall term, ending what then seemed to be another dead-end venture outside the family business.

Rather than send Brian back to armchairs and cocktail tables, Harry teamed him with Clive for a new spin-off business, North End Music Stores (NEMS), devoted to domestic and electronic goods. Clive was responsible for the hardware department, including washing machines and radios. Brian was put in charge of the record section. He was responsible for the selection, purchase and in-store promotional display of recordings from all genres. He developed a keen ear for anticipating pop music hits and ordering stock accordingly. In short order NEMS became the place in Liverpool to find music and the store developed a reputation for unrivaled customer service. This included "listening booths" that allowed customers to preview discs before purchase, which made the well-stocked NEMS stores a favorite teen hangout. Young fans could commandeer a booth and sample the latest releases. It was also NEMS policy to guarantee to provide any record that a customer requested. And it was this promise that led Epstein to take notice of the local group with the odd name playing in the club down the road.

Now a confident businessman, he was looking for a bridge that would bring him back over to the artistic world. His sights were set on a life beyond

Liverpool: He just hadn't yet worked out how to get there. In some ways, says Geller, his vision of a better life was a legacy of his Jewish upbringing. "He reflected the attitude of Jewish immigrants that each generation would become more successful. They would look to America, especially New York, with a bit of envy; success there became a goal. This was especially true in show business. America had its own kind of glamour. Epstein was not provincial. He was cosmopolitan. Local success was not enough for him. He could envision more."

• • •

THE LITTLE-KNOWN BAND and its first-time manager had found each other at the perfect time. *The Beatles* had reached the glass ceiling for rock 'n' roll bands in Liverpool. In Eppy, as they called him, *The Beatles* had found a manager with integrity and honor, primed to devote himself to their success in a way no one else could.

"Brian fused everything," says Nat Weiss. "*The Beatles* were together before they met Brian and they had the talent. But it was Brian who was the emotional and psychological catalyst. He had the vision to say that *The Beatles* would be bigger than Elvis in 1961."

Epstein treated his band with respect; in return, they listened to him. "He was in charge and they did what he said," George Martin, the man who would later become their producer, told Geller. "I mean, he was their only hope."

His first task was to recast their image. He had their hair styled, and took them out of the leather jackets and put them into finely tailored mohair suits. On stage, he insisted that they look and act like professionals. They started showing up to gigs on time, stopped drinking and smoking on stage, began to play from a set song list and added an endearing polite bow in unison at the end of each performance. "I think the [RADA] theatre training—and Brian's immersion in pop at the record store—is what made him aware of the potential for the group—style, clothing and so on," says Alan Swerdlow, a friend of the Epstein family.

Next, Epstein began making trips to London to pitch *The Beatles* to record companies. But landing a record contract was a formidable challenge. Epstein had to convince the major labels in London to even consider looking at Liverpool for talent. "It was Epstein's credibility as a major record retailer that got anyone to give him the courtesy of a listen at all when he was first trying to get *The Beatles* a contract," says Geller. "His retail business was important to them."

The Beatles were rejected by nearly every major label. "The boys won't go, Mr. Epstein," Epstein recalled Decca executives telling him. "We know these things. You have a good record business in Liverpool. Stick to that." Only his polished manner and persistent follow-up kept the process going. Epstein wasn't so easily dissuaded. Nerve-wracking as the search was, he continued his pursuit, all while maintaining his responsibilities at NEMS.

Although they were as supportive as usual, his parents were afraid that their eldest son, having finally become a responsible businessman, was foolishly risking his career on behalf of four non-entities. They were troubled by his foray into Liverpool's raucous and less-than-respectable music scene. Their concern was warranted. Epstein's intense commitment to *The Beatles* did have its dark side according to Epstein friend and business associate Peter Brown. "This is when he started taking amphetamines," Brown told Geller.

The Beatles got their big break when Epstein was introduced to the music publisher for EMI Company at a record shop in London. Although the group had already been rejected by three of the four main labels at EMI, the publisher—Sid Coleman—directed him to George Martin, the producer and A&R [artist and repertoire] director of the fourth and smaller jazz and comedy label—Parlophone. Martin was impressed with the young manager. "[Epstein] certainly wasn't cast in the mould of hardened professional. He seemed to be a little bit ingenuous but he was fresh," Martin has said. "I liked him. I thought he was good and I was persuaded by his enthusiasm." This meeting led to *The Beatles'* first test recording session on June 6, 1962, less than six months after Epstein had signed on as their manager.

Martin liked what he heard and offered to sign them, with one proviso: He felt Pete Best's drumming wasn't up to par and planned to use a studio drummer. That clinched a growing desire by Lennon, McCartney and Harrison to replace their band mate, and they left it to their manager to deliver the news. On August 16, 1962, Pete Best was out and Ringo Starr, the drummer for another popular Liverpool band—Rory Storm and the Hurricanes—was in.

The Beatles, as we know them, recorded their first single the following month. On October 5, 1962, Parlophone released "Love Me Do." Brian Epstein and *The Beatles* began their wild ride. After years of dreaming, the five young men stepped together into a film running on fast forward. When "Love Me Do" reached number 17 on the British charts, they were overjoyed.

Though he'd gotten himself closer to the stage, Epstein could still only circle the spotlight. "Brian was a failed creative person," says Geller. "*The Beatles* were successful performers. Brian envied that; he was a wistful admirer. He wanted to be an artist, not a manager. But he also had the self-awareness to see the difference between what you can do and what you'd like to do. He chose what he could do. He propelled them."

Sometime alongside this flourishing business relationship, a deep personal bond had formed between Eppy and his boys. In 1962, Lennon's girlfriend, Cynthia Powell, became pregnant. Aware that the band's appeal depended in part on the "availability" of its members, Epstein quietly arranged the wedding and gave them his flat in Liverpool. When Julian Lennon was born, Epstein was named his godfather, and would later be best man for both Harrison and Starr.

"We all liked him," Cynthia Lennon has said, "because he was so obviously genuine. He had a sunshine face, manners and was very sweet, a gentleman. He was much older than us mentally. I held him a little in awe because I'd never met 'a Brian' before. He had life all sussed out, it seemed to us. He had suits and ties that matched."

Although Epstein never played favorites, he had a clear affection for John. There are lingering rumors that he was in love with Lennon and that their relationship was consummated during a vacation the two took together in Spain shortly after Cynthia gave birth to Julian. Most friends, including other Beatles, have said that this is simply untrue. Lennon was a confirmed heterosexual, and Epstein wouldn't have crossed professional boundaries.

Lennon was a captivating man and it is not outside of the realm of possibility that Epstein was physically attracted to him, says British rock journalist Steve Turner, author of *The Gospel According to The Beatles*.

"Epstein liked rougher people, he liked being taunted and being treated in a cruel way," he says. "There was something in him that drove him to this: Maybe he came to see abuse as something that he deserved. John did have that kind of wicked way of talking."

Lennon was known for biting remarks made at everyone's expense, and he did not spare Epstein, whom he is said to have admired and liked greatly. In "Baby, You're a Rich Man", Lennon is reported to have sung 'Baby you are rich fag Jew' at the end of the record," says Turner. There were other such jibes over the years but Lennon, wrote Coleman, may have been the Beatle who truly grasped the extraordinary qualities in Epstein that made him the driving force behind the group. "Epstein put up with Lennon's remarks. Anyone working with Lennon learned to live with his caustic tongue."

In February 1963, *The Beatles'* second single "Please Please Me" hit number one and the following month their first album began its 30-week stint at the top of the charts. Fame was quick to follow. "It happened suddenly and dramatically," wrote Epstein, "And we weren't prepared for it."

On November 4, 1963, the band received its highest recognition to date: An invitation to play for Queen Elizabeth and her family at the annual Royal Command Performance. Deferring to Epstein's judgment, Lennon agreed to clean up a planned humorous remark directed at the royal family in which he invited them to rattle "your jewelry" rather than your "fucking jewelry." The expletive-free version went over well and the band was a hit. Princess Margaret was smitten.

The Beatles now had broad appeal throughout Britain. "Without Brian *The Beatles* never get out of Liverpool," says Glenn Frankel, a former *Washington Post* reporter who spent months in the British port city researching Epstein's life. "Liverpool was a small subsidiary of the Empire. It was Podunk and people in London looked down their noses at Liverpool talent. There was no way to get from here to here to there. Without Brian they could have been Michelangelo but they didn't get out. Without Brian, they were just the best band in Liverpool."

· · ·

IN LESS THAN ONE YEAR, *The Beatles* went from releasing their first record to being the number one act in England. The British press coined the term

"Beatlemania" to describe the fanatic reception the group received in public. Epstein's role for the group took on a new aspect. It was only a few months ago that Epstein was knocking on doors to sell *The Beatles*. Now, he was their first line of defense, guarding them from incessant press exposure and mobs of excited fans. Under his watchful eye, Epstein guided the "Fab Four" through the whirlwind they were creating.

During it all, Epstein transformed NEMS into a full-fledged talent management company, hired a staff and signed on other talented Liverpool artists such as Gerry and the Pacemakers and Cilla Black. Elvis Presley's manager, Col. Tom Parker, was astonished that Epstein found the time to manage more than one major group. But no matter how many artists Epstein had to juggle, *The Beatles* were always his first love.

Epstein had his eye on America but his connections were limited to the United Kingdom. In the autumn of 1963, New Yorker Sid Bernstein called him at home in Liverpool to ask if *The Beatles* might be interested in playing Carnegie Hall. Bernstein was a music business student at the New School for Social Research and while he hadn't heard the group's music, he'd studied British newspapers for a class. Mention of *The Beatles* had simply been impossible to miss.

Bernstein offered Epstein $6,500 for two shows and Epstein was impressed. According to Coleman, he couldn't wait to tell his friends at Isow's, a Jewish restaurant in London's Soho district where agents socialized. For Bernstein, it was always a pleasure to do business with Epstein. "Once he gave his word he never changed terms or renegotiated."

The two made deals on the phone, not relying on written contracts. "It was like a handshake on the phone. He just had that kind of quality, you believed him, you trusted him. That isn't true of very many people in the business. My experience has taught me that it is very few and far between that you find someone like Brian."

Bernstein and Epstein planned the concerts, and in November, Epstein flew to New York and arranged the three now-famous *Beatles* appearances on *The Ed Sullivan Show*. Their first show still ranks as one of the most viewed programs on American television ever. By the end of 1964, *The Beatles* had replicated their British success in the United States and were the top performers in the nation. "Not only did he get them to the United

Kingdom," says Frankel, "He got them to America. No British pop act had ever succeeded in doing that. They were the first to cross over."

Now that *The Beatles* were a worldwide phenomenon, the time had come for all five men to leave Liverpool. NEMS moved into flashy new offices near the London Palladium. Epstein bought a townhouse at 24 Chapel Street in Belgravia.

It was a heady time for Eppy and the boys. London in the 1960s was a happening place and the band fit right in. They released films such as *A Hard Day's Night* and *Help!*, and in 1965, they were knighted as Members of the British Empire (MBE). Epstein simply glowed when *The Beatles* received their MBEs and Paul McCartney announced that MBE really stood for "Mister Brian Epstein."

Some have speculated that Epstein believed that he was excluded from the honor because he was a homosexual and a Jew, but most say he never expected to be knighted. By now Epstein was a secular Jew who was observant only when in the company of his family, but he never hid his religion. "Once in a while people would make a remark that was anti-Semitic," recalls Weiss. "He would say, 'I am Jewish.' He spoke out against anti-Semitism. He'd get very angry. He was against all prejudices."

As *The Beatles* matured musically in the studio, Epstein arranged ever-larger venues for their live shows. Stops on the 1966 international tour in Japan and the Philippines were especially exhausting, marred with misadventures that were out of Epstein's control. It was, however, the U.S. segment of the tour that threatened to be dangerous.

It all started with a Lennon interview that made American headlines right before *The Beatles* were due to arrive in the States. "Christianity will go," Lennon had said while discussing the state of world religion with a reporter from the *London Evening Standard*. "It will vanish and shrink. I needn't argue with that; I'm right and I will be proved right. We're more popular than Jesus now; I don't know which will go first, rock 'n' roll or Christianity. Jesus was all right but his disciples were thick and ordinary. It's them twisting it that ruins it for me."

Lennon's words set off a storm of outrage in the United States. Demonstrators burned *Beatles* albums and Epstein was afraid that Lennon would be assassinated. "After Lennon made those remarks," recalls Weiss, "Epstein wanted to cancel the whole tour, I met him at the airport and he asked me how much it would cost to cancel. I said about one million. He wanted to pay it. He didn't want anything to happen to them and for them to be exposed to violence. And he wanted to make sure that anyone who had invested in the tour wouldn't lose money." The tour went on, stopping at stadium venues from Chicago to San Francisco.

When *The Beatles* came home they decided to exclusively focus on studio recording and went to work on one their seminal albums—*Sergeant Pepper's Lonely Hearts Club Band.* Epstein loved touring and was disappointed by the band's decision, but ever supportive, he helped launch the album with a party at his London residence.

Epstein was the glue that kept the foursome focused as they redefined popular music. "*The Beatles* followed him and believed in Brian," says Bernstein. "He handled himself so beautifully and reduced what might have been huge problems to 'Let's get on with it, boys,' and they did. It's always tough keeping a group together. Each band member has his own problems and multiply it fourfold. But he kept them together, unified and they followed his recommendations to the letter."

Even without touring, there was more than enough to keep Epstein busy. "There were so many deals, important deals," says Bernstein. "His phones never stopped and the proposals given to him were of an enormous, enormous nature and enormous amounts of money."

In hindsight, Epstein has been criticized for failing to secure the most lucrative deals for *The Beatles* during the 1960s. "It was a different era," says Turner. "Bands today realize that they can make as much money from T-shirts, programs and spin-off products. But in those days, they didn't know it." Epstein was one of the first band managers to deal with merchandising contracts. "He really almost gave stuff away."

Overall, *The Beatles* were pleased with Epstein's management style and understanding of his shortcomings. "The problem arose because…he hadn't done this kind of business before," said Paul McCartney in *In My Life*. "He had a great theatricality. But I think some of the deals he got us were great for the time but not so great, it turned out… I think for what he knew and for what he could bring us, he was really excellent, and I don't think *The Beatles* would have been the same without him…He was the director. That's what he really was."

Epstein's value to *The Beatles* could not be measured by money, says Weiss: "I don't think that what *The Beatles* needed was a great businessman. They needed a person who would inspire them, whose neurosis was sufficient for him to identify with them. And for Brian *The Beatles* were an alter ego. Brian was on stage with those *Beatles* emotionally and he devoted his life to them."

• • •

THE PRESSURE OF STAYING on top of the music world was relentless. The pill-popping habit that began when Epstein was first pitching *The Beatles* grew worse. He became dependent on sleeping pills and suffered from insomnia, depression and excessive irritability. He took drugs to stay up at night and sleep away the day.

Despite Epstein's manic hours and drug abuse, he made sure to pull himself together when he visited with his family, says Weiss. He remained especially close to his mother. "She had great taste and he had great taste. She was a very sophisticated lady, almost aristocratic in her bearing." Mother and son discussed everything, including his relationships with men and her hope that he would one day get married. Joe Flannery says that Epstein "was also attracted to ladies, and I am saying ladies, and they were attracted to him. There was one, Alma Cogan [born Alma Angela Cohen], a huge star in the 1950s. He was very fond of her and she of him. Remember, he was very young. He was very busy and he didn't really have any time for long-term relationships. If he hadn't died he probably would have had a [long-term] relationship [with a man] by now. And a wife."

On July 7, 1967, Harry Epstein died at the age of 63. Brian Epstein was at Queenie's side within hours of the death and made the arrangements. "The loss of his father shattered Brian," wrote Coleman. "The years of pre-*Beatles* misunderstanding had been replaced by Harry's pride in his eldest son's achievements and fame. On the return from the cemetery to the new Epstein home in Woolton, he sobbed uncontrollably in the car."

Epstein stayed with Queenie at her house during the week of shiva. Away from the world of *The Beatles*, he found time for reflection. "My father's passing has given me the added responsibility of my mother," he wrote his friend Nat Weiss. "The week of shiva is up tonight and I feel a bit strange. Probably been good for me in a way. Time to think and note that at least now I'm really needed by Mother. Also time to note that the unworldly Jewish circle of my parents' and brother's friends are not so bad. Provincial, maybe, but warm, sincere and basic."

For the next three weekends Epstein traveled to Liverpool to be close to his mother. When he was away he phoned her every night, and on August 14th, she came to London for a 10-day visit, during which he comforted and lavishly entertained her. "He rose at early times and went bed at a normal time, a routine refreshingly different for him," wrote Coleman. They made plans for Queenie to move to London so that she could be near him.

Two days after she left, on August 25th, he drove up to his new five-acre 18th century country home—Kingsley Hill. He dined with friends Peter Brown and Geoffrey Ellis, and then waited for some guests he had invited for the evening. When they didn't show, he drove back to his home in London.

The next morning several friends made calls to Epstein's house but received no answer. When no one heard from him by evening, they became alarmed and broke down to his bedroom door. They found his body, still in bed. Next to him was a pile of open correspondence, a working script for *The Beatles* movie *Yellow Submarine* and a book he was reading, *The Rabbi*, by Noah Gordon.

The coroner's report ruled his death accidental, the result of an overdose of the sedative Carbirtal. Brian's brother, Clive, and his wife Barbara, then eight months pregnant, got the call and were the ones to break the news to Queenie. Still in mourning, she had sustained another unthinkable loss. "The poor woman was devastated at having lost her husband and son within three months," says Weiss.

The Beatles were on retreat with Maharishi Mahesh Yogi, spiritual leader and founder of the Transcendental Meditation movement, in Wales, when they were notified. "It was just like one of those phone calls: 'Brian's dead,'" recalled McCartney. "You just sort of went pale and immediately traipsed off to the Maharishi. We said, 'Our friend is dead. How do we handle this?' And he gave us practical advice. 'Nothing you can do. Bless him, wish him well, get on with life' kind of thing. But we were very shocked and what added to it, as it always does with celebrities, the media wanted to know how you feel and it's always too quick...you just can't talk about it."

Rumors spread that Epstein committed suicide but his friends and family never believed this likely. There was no note or legal will, and Epstein had many plans for the future. Most of all, he was devoted to his mother, who needed him more than ever at the time of his death.

The family wanted a quiet Orthodox funeral at the Greenbank Drive Synagogue and asked *The Beatles* not to attend for fear that it would draw too much public attention. Following Orthodox tradition, only the men accompanied Epstein's body to the Jewish Cemetery on Long Lane in Aintree. Epstein was buried near his father. "After the burial, the rabbi, who didn't know Brian, said something about him being a symbol of the malaise of his generation, which was amazing," says Weiss. "How can a man who filled stadiums, who literally was the catalyst for the greatest musical event of the 20th century, be treated as a malaise of his generation? It was such an unjust epitaph. It was disgusting."

Six weeks later, *The Beatles* attended a memorial service at the New London Synagogue on Abbey Road. All four wore black paper yarmulkes. This time the officiating rabbi, Louis Jacobs, praised Epstein, "He encouraged young people," Jacobs said, "to sing of love and peace rather than war and hatred."

· · ·

IN THE MONTHS AFTER EPSTEIN'S DEATH, *The Beatles* would come to realize what they already suspected: Brian Epstein was irreplaceable. Without him, John Lennon, Paul McCartney, George Harrison and Ringo Starr had no one they trusted to look out for their interests. Without Epstein's unique combination of ethics, protectiveness and charm, they were forced to handle business details and interpersonal squabbles by themselves.

There was no obvious successor. McCartney, then engaged to Linda Eastman, supported her brother, Lee, a lawyer, for the role. (Eastman's family was Jewish; coincidentally, Eastman was an anglicized version of their original name, Epstein.) The other was Allen Klein, an established rock manager who handled such acts as *The Rolling Stones*. Klein did take care of some key record company negotiations and reorganized the new company that *The Beatles* had formed—Apple—with the blessing of Lennon, Harrison and Starr, but McCartney never signed on.

The Fab Four began managing themselves but without their long-time friend and mediator, the atmosphere grew increasingly acrimonious. In his book *Here, There, and Everywhere*, studio engineer Geoff Emerick remembered the 1968 sessions for what became *The Beatles*, most commonly called *The White Album*, being painfully difficult, as interpersonal tensions spilled into the studio. Viewers of the theatrical feature *Let It Be*, filmed during recording sessions held in early 1969, could see the tension for themselves on screen.

Even as the band identity that Epstein had so carefully crafted began to disappear, the momentum he had helped build continued. From 1967 to 1970, *The Beatles* went on to produce some of their greatest music, including "Hey Jude," their most successful single, and *Abbey Road*, one of their most respected albums. But the old feeling was gone. "We made a few more albums but we were sort of winding up," said McCartney. "We always felt we'd come full circle and Brian's death was part of it." In 1970, less than three years after Epstein passed away, *The Beatles* disbanded. "After Brian died, we collapsed," said Lennon in a 1971 *Rolling Stone* interview.

· · ·

THERE ARE FEW REMINDERS of Brian Epstein left in Liverpool. A plaque and an oil portrait hang in the lobby of the Neptune Theater, which is currently closed for remodeling. Photographs and notes about Epstein line the wall of "*The Beatles* Story Exhibition."

Outside of town is the small Jewish cemetery where the Epstein family plot can be found. "It's the saddest thing," says Glenn Frankel, who visited the cemetery recently. "Brian had finally escaped Liverpool and was back before he was 33. Clive died of a heart attack in 1988 at the age of fifty-one. And there is Queenie, who survived all her men and who was pretty miserable at the end of her life, having her golden family fall away."

The epitaph on Epstein's tombstone does not say anything about his life accomplishments. The grave is simple, says Weiss, as befits a man whom he calls a good Jew. "Brian adhered to the best tenets of Judaism, he kept to the highest values of the Jewish faith," he says. "He was an honest man, extremely fair in his dealings. He was very compassionate and understanding of his fellow man, he believed in mercy and compassion. He was very kind and very generous. He was like a saint in that respect." ͡

9

UNCLE XENON:
THE ELEMENTAL OLIVER SACKS
Nadine Epstein • January/February 2008

OLIVER SACKS OPENS THE DOOR of his lower Manhattan apartment himself because his assistant, Kate Edgar, is in the emergency room with a twisted ankle. He looks somewhat befuddled, although he is expecting us. He is neither tall nor short, slightly round in the middle and wearing a button-down shirt, one middle button undone. His shyness, which is legendary, is evident from the moment he greets us, as he steps back awkwardly to make room for us to come inside.

My 15-year-old son Noah is with me, skipping school for the opportunity to meet the writer of *The Man Who Mistook his Wife for a Hat, An Anthropologist on Mars*, the new *Musicophilia: Tales of Music and the Brain* and other volumes. Using the old-fashioned but powerful technique of medical narrative, with patients as heroes, Sacks' work has bridged the divide between modern science and the human soul, stirring the curiosity of the general public. With prodigious literary skill, his anecdotal books illuminate tales of the brain's misfunctions, and, on occasion, its amazing ability to compensate.

In large white Nikes, Sacks pads across the living room-turned-office, passing by Kate's empty desk. "I am so very worried about her," he tells us earnestly in an accent that has been described as from Jewish North London (where he grew up) with shades of Oxford (where he studied). He leads us into a smaller office, an inner sanctum. Sacks shuns computers, so a bulky electric typewriter sits waiting in the sunlight that pours in through the window.

Sacks has never married and is said to have given up on committed romantic relationships. He has no children of his own but has many young relatives and godchildren, not to mention numerous correspondents under the age of ten; it's clear that Noah's presence comes as a relief. He shows us his bulletin board (which he calls a "notice board"), plastered with photographs and other mementoes. He is 74; the corkboard is full. With evident pleasure he points to photographs of a few of his patients, some of whom he has written into life in his books and *New Yorker* articles. These are tacked haphazardly among pictures of his intellectual heroes, like chemists Linus Pauling and Michael Faraday and the late naturalist Stephen Jay Gould, his dear friend. "I had a dream about him last night," Sacks says. "As you get older and people die, they get into your dreams more and more."

Noah and I have carefully crafted questions to ask Sacks, but neither of us wants to interrupt this near-breathless show-and-tell. A fossil resting on his desk now carries him to the subject of stromatolites, colonies of photosynthetic bacteria that filled the atmosphere with oxygen three billion or so years ago. "When I get tired of the modern world, I imagine the Archaean world when stromatolites were the only signs of life," he remarks. Stromatolites were long thought to be extinct, but luckily for Sacks, living ones were found in Australia. "I sat by them for three days, just watching them bubble oxygen, trying to form a relationship with them," he says.

He begins to move around his office, showing us his collection of representations of the Periodic Table, including one shaped like a Hanukkah menorah that was drawn by a young correspondent. In his 2001 book, *Uncle Tungsten: Memories of a Chemical Boyhood*, Sacks reveals his obsession with the chemical elements, especially with heavy metals. "I feel I commune with my uranium and tungsten," he explains.

On his desk lie actual chunks of elements in all shapes and sizes. He sits in his swivel chair and hands us a small tablet of gold to caress. Other metals follow. "When people have birthdays, I give them elements," he says as we take turns holding each specimen. "Tin is element 50 and since ten people have turned 50 lately, I'm out of tin. A good friend of mine was 80 recently and I said to him, 'I wish you were 79, because then I could have given you something made of gold, but since you're 80, I have to enclose a bottle of mercury.' I'm waiting for one elderly friend to be 83 so I can give him some bismuth." For his own 65th birthday, Sacks had balloons filled with xenon (though it is element #54), which is five times denser than air. "I loved these balloons," he says. "One normally thinks of balloons going up, but these balloons came down and fell on the ground like cushions."

Sacks tries not to discriminate among elements any more than he would pick favorites among godchildren, but he can't hide his affection for noble gases, formerly known as inert gases, and for element #54 in particular. "I'm rather fond of xenon," he admits, "partly because it's so rare, partly because its name means stranger. But specifically, it was the first inert gas to be persuaded to combine with other elements. So at the point when someone as solitary as myself is finally tipped into relationship and community, then I feel like xenon."

According to family lore, Sacks' grandfathers were so Orthodox that one would wake up at night if his yarmulke slipped off his head while the other would not swim without his. Sacks himself was raised in an illustrious Jewish clan in London. His parents' spacious house on Mapesbury Road was strictly kosher, and the family—four boys, of which he was the youngest—regularly attended shul together. But for the Sacks family, Judaism revolved around family and tradition rather than belief. As a child, he delighted in the Shema, lighting Shabbat candles with his mother, the rituals of the Seder and especially Sukkot, when the family built a sukkah in the garden.

Although the Sacks household was always filled with cousins, uncles and aunts, some of whom wore sheitls and were, in his words, "excessively Orthodox," the dominant culture was not of religion, but of science. Sacks' mother Elsie was a surgeon who later specialized in gynecology and obstetrics; to teach Oliver about the brain she dissected malformed fetuses at home. His father Samuel, a popular family doctor who made house calls, had set aside his dream of becoming a neurologist. Many relatives were scientifically inclined, among them his mother's brother Dave Landau, the eponymous Uncle Tungsten, who, in addition to his abiding interest in chemistry, owned a factory that manufactured tungsten light bulbs. The scientific streak dates back to the 17th century, when one of Sacks' ancestors was an "alchemical rabbi," practicing the ancient pseudoscience of alchemy—the predecessor to chemistry.

Until he was six, Oliver's life was near perfect. That was when his parents sent him and his older brother Michael to the country to keep them safe from Luftwaffe bombs. Beginning in 1939, the boys spent four years in a makeshift boarding school in the Midlands where, unbeknownst to their family, they subsisted on meager rations of turnips and beetroot and suffered cruel punishments at the hands of a sadistic headmaster.

Everyone in the family survived the war, but Oliver and Michael emerged scarred. Michael eventually became psychotic, but the troubled Oliver was saved from a similar fate by the comfort he found in the visual ordering of elements that came to Russian chemist Dmitri Mendeleev in an 1869 dream: the Periodic Table. Sacks vividly recalls the awe and reverence he felt the first time he visited the Science Museum in South Kensington after the war and saw his first representation of the Periodic Table, covering an entire wall. "The Periodic Table was an irrefutable confirmation that there was cosmic order in the universe," he has said, adding that he identified Mendeleev with Moses "coming down from Sinai with the tablets of the periodic law."

Encouraged by his family, he set up a home laboratory in which he found the behavior of the elements of endless interest. "First there are the qualities: the colors, the smells, the fusings, the bubblings," he says. "Then there's a special fascination when you find the quantitative, when you find, shall we say, 23 grams of sodium [and] 35.5 of chlorine make salt. Then there's another grade of excitement when you think at the atomic level and realize that sodium has an extra electron which it needs to get rid of, whereas chlorine is avid to get an electron because it only has seven. The two of them meet and sodium says 'Hey, you take it!' and the chlorine grabs it. It's a marriage made in heaven."

Later, when Sacks chose to study medicine at Oxford, he was transfixed by the chemistry of the brain, leading him to the clinical study of neurology. But after graduating in 1960, Sacks was a failure at medical research; his studies of human nutrition were "disastrous," he once told the British newspaper *The Guardian*. He traveled to Canada, ostensibly on vacation, and sent a telegram to his parents with nothing more than the word, "Staying." (He announced an intention to become a U.S. citizen 46 years ago but "never got 'round to it.") He made his way to California, eventually taking a position as a neurologist at UCLA. During this period, he also began to pursue another dream, of being a writer.

In 1966, he switched coasts, joining the Albert Einstein College of Medicine in New York. More attempts at research were disappointing, he told

The Guardian: "I lost samples. I broke machines. Finally they said to me, 'Sacks, you're' a menace. Get out. Go see patients. They matter less.'"

Of course, it was his feeling that patients did not matter less that was to make Sacks such an insightful clinician and writer. In 1970, he published a book on migraines, an affliction he had suffered from during his youth. Three years later he published *Awakenings,* based on his experience with a group of patients at Beth Abraham Hospital in the Bronx. Most of them poor elderly Jews, they had been immobilized for decades by a Parkinsonian torpor as a result of contracting encephalitis during a global epidemic in the 1920s.

Sacks was touched by these patients, written off as incurable by the medical establishment. In *Awakenings,* later made into a film starring Robin Williams as Sacks, he recounts their unorthodox treatment with an experimental drug called L-dopa, with which he roused them, temporarily, to full consciousness. But not until *The Man Who Mistook His Wife for a Hat* in 1988 did Sacks become a popular sensation, revered for his storytelling and ability to make understandable the complex orchestration of neurons and synapses that comprise the brain. "He makes very thoughtful clinical observations and looks for patients with similar syndromes," says Columbia University neuroscientist Eric Kandel. Kandel recently helped persuade Sacks to leave his longtime post at Albert Einstein to join Columbia's faculty, and become its first interdisciplinary "university artist."

"At heart I'm sort of a naturalist of everything from minerals and plants and animals to human beings and human experiences," Sacks says. "I want to know what it's like to be someone who's blind or having hallucinations or hearing music, although I would also like to know what goes on in their brain while that's happening. What could be more interesting than the brain and mind?"

• • •

SITTING IN HIS OFFICE, fully immersed in the delightful multitudinous stream issuing forth from Sacks' brain, we lose all sense of time and space. Finally, Noah asks a question that is not on our list—"What is your favorite kind of bagel?"—that leads Sacks to Judaism, not among his favorite subjects. "In general I don't talk to people about religion, any more than I talk to them about politics or sex," he tells us. "I think those are all dangerous subjects, charged with unreason."

But Sacks is happy to divulge that he loves pumpernickel bagels, especially "topped with herring." Naturally, the topic veers to smoked salmon, which was a favorite of Sacks'—along with Bach—when he was five. "I still say much the same," he adds with a laugh.

One of the photographs he shows us is of his first cousin, Sir Robert John Aumann, a mathematician awarded the 2005 Nobel Prize in economics for game theory. Aumann is Orthodox; it was he who gave Sacks the mezuzah that hangs on his apartment door. Sacks is an atheist. "Personally, I do not feel any need for religious belief," he says. "On the other hand, I respect other people's need for it." He celebrates holidays with friends and, although he rarely attends shul, has a preference for Orthodox services held in Hebrew, which he considers a "sacred language."

"Judaism is a profoundly historical religion," he says. "A profoundly ethical one." But he fears religious intolerance, and doesn't find Judaism exempt. "I consider religious fanaticism more likely than anything else to combine with technology to destroy the planet," he says.

It is, in part, his disdain for extremism of any kind that keeps him distant from Israel. In 1955, he spent three wonderful months there, visiting Jerusalem, Tsfat and Eilat, where he made his first primitive but joyous scuba dive. He also stayed on a kibbutz near Haifa called Ain ha Shafet. "I enjoyed the unworldly idealistic communal life in the kibbutz," he says. "It was good for the xenon part of me. It was a healthy, important experience for a solitary intellectual, pathologically shy person to work on a farm, do physical work and be in the community."

But he has felt out of sympathy with Israel since 1967, when it came into possession of the territories. His feelings, he admits, have also been influenced by personal matters. His mother died there, and he believes that another of his first cousins—the late Israeli Ambassador to the United States, Foreign Minister and Deputy Prime Minister Abba Eban—was sidelined because he was not sufficiently partisan. "He was a man deeply versed in Arabic literature and I think, increasingly in the 1960s, when things hardened in Israel, the whiff of his sympathies itself became ground for suspicion," says Sacks.

Sacks has never returned to Israel but once considered traveling to an

Arab village on the West Bank where a fifth of the population is born clinically deaf and villagers, hearing and deaf alike, communicate in sign language. He eventually decided against it, although he liked the idea of a visit for medical research. "I'm a great believer in being non-political and nonpartisan."

Talking about religion and politics seems to drain Sacks, but when the topic returns to chemistry, his eyes regain their twinkle. A self-styled chemistry "evangelist," he takes it upon himself to supply his many young relatives and friends with periodic tables. "Uncle Oliver has become like Uncle Tungsten that way," he muses. Noah wants to know if he still maintains a home lab. He doesn't, but can't resist the occasional home chemistry experiment. "Kate came in one day and found me melting some sulfur in the microwave," he recalls. "It caught fire and the whole place was full of sulfur dioxide."

The phone rings in the outer office, jarring us all. Sacks, hoping it might be Kate reporting from the emergency room, leaps to answer. But it is clearly not his beloved assistant. When he reenters his office, he is flustered and cursing. A reporter who recently spoke with him about *Musicophilia* wants to re-interview him because her recorder didn't work. "I can't remember what I've said once I've said it!" he tells us, astonished at her audacity. He glances over at me to make sure I am taking notes, which I am. Then Sacks looks warily in the direction of Noah and our recorder.

"The fact is that the basic skills of journalism, which are pen and paper, are being forgotten," he mutters. "I'm very concerned about the disappearance of skills which have survived for a long while. My father was very good at percussing the chest and listening, and could learn a huge amount from this," he continues. "It is important to know the old way of examining someone, the hands-on way."

This leads him to an account of a recent conference on the subject of communications. "I'm shy in panels and conferences, but occasionally I want to say something, and at one point someone said that his little daughter is online all the while—I broke in and said that I was horrified. 'Doesn't she ever read a book?' I asked."

One word, he says, was missing from the discussion. "The word was solitude," Sacks says. "Everyone was speaking about speed and the Web and bandwidth and information transfer, but so much of the world's real work depends on solitary thinking and depth."

The phone rings again. This time it is Kate. "Are you in a lot of pain?" he asks her. She is, but even so, ever his caretaker, reminds him it is time to ask us to leave. As soon as he hangs up the phone, he does so. "I'm a babbler," he says, apologetically, adding that the Babylon Talmud is sometimes called the Talmud Babli.

He stands up and walks to the door, without giving me time to gather my notes or for Noah to disentangle the wires of the recorder. "Sorry to be so abrupt," he says as we scramble to follow. "Every minute I spend with you keeps me away from my work." The door closes behind us, ending a glorious morning with Uncle Xenon, a truly noble element.

IN MEMORY OF WARREN DENNIS

MOMENT DEDICATES *NINE LIVES* to the memory of Warren L. Dennis. Warren was a prominent lawyer whose work ranged from defending bankers and corporate giants to representing the homeless, Secret Service agents, missing and abused children and the NAACP Legal Fund. Warren began practicing law in 1972 in the Justice Department's Civil Rights Division. While there, he chaired the division's task force on financing discrimination and helped initiate government enforcement programs in connection with sex discrimination in lending and racial redlining. Later, Warren was a senior partner at the law firm of Proskauer Rose, LLP and a leader of the National Center for Missing and Exploited Children. A community activism enthusiast, Warren co-founded Project Shelter for the homeless in Washington DC. He was deeply committed to *Moment* and chaired its advisory board until he passed away in 2004 at the age of 55.

AFTERWORDS

I met Warren Dennis because of his love of justice. He was working against housing discrimination in the Civil Rights Division of the U.S. Department of Justice; a division then headed by our mutual friend, Stan Pottinger. Because Diane Dennis was also an innovative activist on this country's need for child-care, the four of us had dinners full of good talk and friendship.

But not until Warren was in private practice in Washington, DC, did I personally experience his kindness and generosity in serving justice. I had come to the end of every avenue I knew in working on a child sexual abuse case, one of too many in which the judge assumed that a vengeful wife must be making false charges against a husband and father. This case was before a judge in Maryland who had never failed to grant unsupervised custody to a father accused of sexually abusing his child, regardless of evidence. Indeed, he refused to let expert witnesses testify, or to allow young survivors to show what they had experienced by using dolls, often the only way they could speak. He ruled his courtroom like an irrational monarch. That was the situation when I asked Warren to become the mother's pro bono lawyer.

At first, Warren also found it hard to believe there was no recourse to legal logic or evidence. Then he put his whole heart and good mind into rescuing this child, her mother, and the siblings who also had been abused, including a daughter who was the child of the father but was being shielded by her stepmother. Not only did Warren win on behalf of the mother, but largely as a result of this case, the biased judge was later removed from the bench.

I have seen the mother over the years, so I know she remains an activist who rescues many other children. She credits Warren with giving her faith that reform in the system was possible, and that some lawyers cared. When she had another daughter in a happy marriage, I was honored that she named her "Gloria," but had that child been a boy, she and I would have been more honored to have another "Warren" in the world.

Judaism calls on all of us to seek justice in this life. Because Warren did this with all his heart, justice lives beyond him.

Gloria Steinem
New York, New York, 2011

* * *

AT THE HOUSE AFTER WARREN'S FUNERAL, I sat and listened to the different things people said about him. I overheard a young associate say that Warren had "lived to win" and that he was a litigator first. He was speaking to a senior partner at the firm who gently corrected him and explained that Warren was about winning but not for the sake of winning. He went on to explain that Warren fought for the underdog, the guy who was being mistreated whether by the government or some huge corporation or some bully representing big business. As I was listening, I flashed back to when we were driving back from the cemetery after his dad's unveiling, and some guys pulled along the side of our car and started screaming anti-Semitic epithets through their window. Warren went crazy. He raced until he caught up with the guys, and I thought he would kill them he was so angry. We were 20 years old, married with a baby, and I saw a side of him that day that would be a common thread throughout our lives. Warren didn't like bullies.

He was raised in South Philadelphia, and he learned early that there was bigotry in the world. We met when we were 15 years old, and even at that young age he talked about the importance of defending the underdog. He was driven to watch all the documentaries about Hitler and studied for hours to figure out what the take away was from this epic tragedy. His years of study confirmed for him that we are all formed from the same cloth and have the responsibility to fight for equality. He started doing just that in the Civil Rights Division of the Justice Department, where he would travel to neighborhoods in the South where residents wouldn't sell their homes to blacks or Jews. He would go after the realtors, bringing lawsuits, and was not happy until he successfully integrated the neighborhoods. He was never afraid, because he knew what he was doing was ultimately fighting the bullies.

Warren continued this work through the Center for Missing and Exploited Children, where he would defend the rights of children against parents with dishonorable motives; through his work with the Anti-Defamation League, where he worked to bring people of all faiths and colors together, and through his efforts to fight the District of Columbia when it was in the process of foreclosing on a children's shelter.

Even more important, he fought silently for the guy who lost his health insurance because he was diagnosed with colon cancer.

Warren was on a mission that was to follow the values of Judaism. He didn't push these tenets on others. He just was committed to living them each day. Seth, Joanna and I were very lucky to take this ride with Warren. He passed way too young, but in his 55 short years he had an impact on a lot of people, including that young associate that day in our living room.

Diane Dennis
McLean, Virginia, 2011

• • •

MY FATHER HAD AN AMAZING CAPACITY FOR LEARNING. He was as knowledgeable in Renaissance art as he was in Rommel's tactics for controlling the German Panzer divisions. He loved learning about Judaism most of all. As a result, he possessed a complex understanding of what it meant to be a Jew. He could talk about Jews in the Middle Ages, how the Jews influenced the Roman Republic, the creation of Israel, the translation of Hebrew to Aramaic, and how that influenced our understanding of the Torah, and how all of these things interacted and were expressed in modern Jewish culture and thought.

He also loved sharing his knowledge with others, and because I was often the closest captive audience, I got to benefit from his understanding of these things. But despite the breadth of what he knew, he described Judaism to me in the same way that Rabbi Hillel described it, standing on one foot: "What is hateful to you, do not do unto your neighbor, the rest is commentary…" For my father, knowledge and facts provided context, but God was found in being kind to others, and that is what I think Judaism meant to him.

Seth Dennis
McLean, Virginia, 2011

• • •

MANY OF YOU WILL REMEMBER Warren Dennis as a board leader and champion of *Moment*, a brilliant lawyer, and an advocate for social justice. However, my brother Warren's connection to Judaism was the essence of everything he did and was; Judaism was his touchstone and his compass. He loved *Moment* because he wanted to share Jewish thought, history and culture from generation to generation. Most important, he wanted to continue the dialogue and enable our rich heritage to live and evolve, so that it would forever remain relevant to our lives today. He was a lifelong student of Judaism and a teacher in every sense of the word. He loved the debate, and while he did not profess to have all the answers, he cherished the search for knowledge and always respected different points of view.

Warren carried our Jewish traditions with him and was the keeper of our family history. He wrote his own Haggadah in the context of current Jewish experience to teach his family about the diaspora's unique relationship to the land of Israel. It is not only a beautiful teaching, but also it relates Jewish struggle and faith to present-day challenges. As Morris Joseph said, "Liberty is the inalienable right of every human being." Warren believed that with all his heart. He was a tireless advocate for social justice and he "repaired the world" with his words and his deeds.

For my brother, Warren, Judaism was tzedakah. He lived it. I remember on Rosh Hashanah that he sent tzedakah banks to all of his extended family. Mine sits in front of me every day as a reminder of Warren's passion to help others. Above all, Warren was "his brother's keeper." He understood his obligation to his family and to the Jewish people. *Moment* gave Warren the opportunity to use his incredible intellect and passion to ensure the continuity of Jewish thought and culture. We are grateful that he was able to make such a contribution.

Robert Dennis
Fair Haven, New Jersey, 2011

ACKNOWLEDGMENTS

DECADES HAVE PASSED SINCE Elie Wiesel and Leonard Fein first engaged America in a critical and independent conversation of Jewish religion, politics and culture. The publishing torch has been passed from generation to generation (many generations, if we honor our namesake *Der Moment,* which was published in Warsaw from 1910 until 1939), but our goal of providing excellence in independent Jewish journalism remains steadfast.

With our mission in mind, we are excited to publish this book, *Nine Lives: Favorite Profiles of Famous People from the Annals of Moment Magazine,* which brings together some of the most brilliant Jewish figures of our time. We must admit that it was difficult to select our favorites. So many amazing people and stories have been featured in *Moment* over the years that we could fill many volumes.

A book such as this—on top of publishing our flagship print edition, digital edition, InTheMoment blog, e-newsletter, and running contests (short fiction, memoir writing, book review writing for nine to 13-year-olds, emerging writers awards, plus more) and holding symposiums and events—requires much love and attention. We are indebted to many, first and foremost the wonderful family of the late Warren Dennis, a man who cared deeply about *Moment* and guided it through difficult times. His wife Diane Lipton Dennis, son Seth and daughter Joanna, and his brother, Robert, supported the publication of *Nine Lives* with their creativity, generosity and love. We also thank the authors of the profiles included in this volume for crafting these fine examples of portrait journalism, no easy task. Some such as Jeremy Gillick, Nonna Gorilovskaya, Rebecca Frankel and David Zax were members of our staff when they wrote these stories. Others such as Mandy Katz, Ted Merwin, Johanna Neuman, Walter J. Podrazik and Abigail Pogrebin were freelance writers. As we at *Moment* know so well, all good stories require more effort than one would imagine, and we are grateful that each writer gave of their time and passion with grace. Thank you also to Andrew Muchin and Rachel Sklar as well as interns and staff members who assisted with research and interviews. Our gratitude extends warmly to the kind and thoughtful Sidney Offit for his fascinating foreword, and Warren's dear friend, Gloria Steinem, for her illuminating afterword.

This book has been a labor of love as is every issue of *Moment*. It would not have been published without the labor and love of those who have worked at *Moment* over the years. Most recently, Leslie Holz assisted with zest as did Sarah Breger, Sala Levin, Niv Elis and Aubrey López. Navid Marvi deftly designed this book with the assistance of Carmen Avila. Still others helped in innumerable ways including *Moment* literary editor Mike Levitas and associate publisher Sarai Brachman Shoup. We thank and honor all of them.

Marcy Epstein
Associate Publisher, Moment Magazine
Ann Arbor, Michigan, 2011

Nadine Epstein
Editor and Publisher, Moment Magazine
Washington, DC, 2011

AUTHORS & CONTRIBUTORS

NADINE EPSTEIN is editor and publisher of *Moment*. Her articles, essays and op-ed pieces have appeared in *The New York Times, The New York Times Magazine, The Washington Post, Smithsonian, The Christian Science Monitor, Ms.* and other publications. She is the co-author of three books and contributor to anthologies including *Racing in the Street: The Bruce Springsteen Reader.*

REBECCA FRANKEL is deputy managing editor of foreignpolicy.com. Prior to joining *Foreign Policy*, she was managing editor of *Moment*. She is the author of the popular feature, "Rebecca's War Dogs of the Week."

JEREMY GILLICK, a *Moment* contributor and former fellow, has written for *The Forward, Tablet* and London's *Jewish Chronicle*. He is currently a graduate student in Jewish and Middle Eastern history at the University of California, Davis, focusing on radical movements in Jewish society and religion.

NONNA GORILOVSKAYA, *Moment*'s editor-at-large, was managing editor of the magazine. A former fellow at *Mother Jones* and recipient of a U.S. Fulbright scholarship to Armenia, she is a doctoral student in politics at the University of Edinburgh, a researcher at Harvard University's NiemanWatchdog.com and author of the Women in Foreign Policy Blog.

MANDY KATZ, a *Moment* contributor and former senior editor, writes for *The New York Times, The Washington Post* and *Cleveland Plain-Dealer*. The author of the 2011 *Moment Magazine Jewish American Heritage Guide*, she also serves as communications officer for Tudor Place Historic House and Garden in Washington, DC.

MARK MALSEED, a former researcher for Bob Woodward on *New York Times* bestsellers *Plan of Attack* and *Bush at War*, is an investigative journalist and information industry consultant. He is co-author of *The Google Story* and co-founder of OhMyGov.com, an award-winning political blog and research firm.

TED MERWIN is a professor, writer and journalist. He is the author of *In Their Own Image: New York Jews in Jazz Age Popular Culture*. He is also the author of a forthcoming book on the history of the Jewish delicatessen, *Pastrami on Rye: An Overstuffed History of the Jewish Deli.*

JOHANNA NEUMAN is a journalist and writer who is currently pursuing her doctorate in history at American University. The author of *Lights, Camera, War*, a 1996 book about the history of media technology, she has been a staff reporter for the *Los Angeles Times, U.S. News & World Report* and *USA Today.*

SIDNEY OFFIT is a novelist, teacher and curator emeritus of the George Polk Journalism Awards. He has served on the Authors Guild Council for three decades and is the President of the Authors Guild Foundation. He is also on the board of PEN American Center. The author of many books, his most recent is *Friends, Writers, and Other Countrymen,* recalls some 60 years of American literary life.

WALTER J. PODRAZIK is a visiting lecturer in communications at the University of Illinois at Chicago, consulting curator at Chicago's Museum of Broadcast Communications, a media planner and analyst, and co-author of 10 books including *Watching TV: Six Decades of American Television* as well as three books on *The Beatles.*

ABIGAIL POGREBIN, a former *60 Minutes* producer, is the author of *Stars of David: Prominent Jews Talk about Being Jewish* and *One and the Same: My Life as an Identical Twin and What I've Learned about Everyone's Struggle to be Singular,* both from Doubleday.

GLORIA STEINEM is a journalist who was the first editor of *Ms.* magazine. A leading activist in the feminist movement since the 1950s, she is also the author of several books including *Outrageous Acts and Everyday Rebellions; Marilyn: Norma Jean; Revolution From Within: A Book of Self-Esteem*; and *Moving Beyond Words.*

DAVID ZAX is a freelance magazine journalist who contributes to *Smithsonian* and a web reporter for *Fast Company*. A former fellow at *Moment*, he has also worked at *The Atlantic* and *Smithsonian,* and has written on science and technology for *Slate, Salon, Wired* and *Seed.*